BULLETIN BOARDS for Children's Ministry

Mary Tucker

STANDARD PUBLISHING™

Cincinnati, Ohio

Bulletin Boards for Children's Ministry

Standard Publishing, Cincinnati, Ohio
A division of Standex International Corporation

© 1999 Standard Publishing Company
All rights reserved
Printed in the United States of America

Credits
Bulletin Boards: Mary Tucker
Cover design: Sandi Welch
Inside illustrations: Daniel A. Grossmann
Project editor: Christine Spence
Acquisitions editor: Ruth Frederick

All Scripture quotations, unless otherwise indicated, are taken from the HOLY BIBLE, NEW
INTERNATIONAL VERSION ®. NIV ®. Copyright © 1973, 1978, 1984 by International Bible
Society. Used by permission of Zondervan Publishing House. All rights reserved.

**Permission is granted to reproduce patterns (pages 142-155) for ministry purposes
only—not for resale.**

06 05 04 03 02 01 00 99   5 4 3 2 1

ISBN 0-7847-0977-7

Contents

contents

Introduction

The following pages contain Bible-based bulletin boards for children of all ages, as well as special holiday and ministry-related boards. Each section of boards begins with an introductory page that explains the special value of the boards for that age group and contains tips for using the boards in the classroom.

To find bulletin boards that deal with a particular Bible character, event, or concept, look in the index in the back of this book. If you use Standard Publishing's Sunday-school curriculum, look at your age group's curriculum syllabus at the end of this book to find boards that correlate with the units you are teaching.

Following is a general list of materials you should have on hand for creating bulletin boards. The instructions for each board will describe any special materials you will need.

Butcher paper
Construction paper
Glue
Markers
Poster board
Scissors
Stapler
Tape
White paper

Block Letter Patterns

Use the instructions below and the patterns on this page to guide you as you cut out letters freehand, or use them to make cardboard patterns.

* The size of paper you use will determine the size of your letters.
* Cut all pieces of paper the same size before you begin. Corners may be rounded, if you prefer.
* For *F*, cut the lower leg off an *E*.
* For *G*, add a tip to a *C*.
* For *Q*, add a slanted tip to the bottom corner of an *O*.
* Cut *E, C, B, D,* and *K* on a horizontal fold. See the bottom of this page.
* Cut *A, H, T, N, O, U, V, W, X,* and *Y* on a vertical fold.
* Do not fold when cutting *I, P, L, J, N, R, S,* and *Z*.

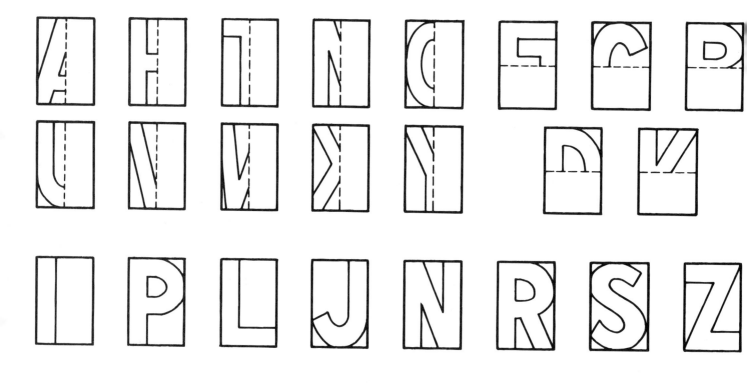

ulletin Boards for Ages 2-4

Young children love visuals. They also love getting involved, so interactive bulletin boards are ideal for teaching God's truths to children ages 2-4. Simple bulletin boards will grab and keep their attention for the few minutes it takes to teach an important concept.

The bulletin boards on the following pages have been designed to communicate to young children. Many of them involve the children in activities that will keep them focused on the lesson or in responses that will help them personalize the truths they learn. As much as possible, try to give children opportunities for putting the boards together. You will need to help with pinning or tacking the pieces on the boards, but the children can place them where they should be. The children's pride in helping is more important than perfect bulletin boards.

If possible, place the bulletin boards low enough on the wall for children to reach them. They not only will want to place items on the boards themselves, but also will want to touch the pieces as you talk about them. Of course, you'll need to make certain rules, such as never removing anything from a bulletin board without the teacher's permission. You may also find the children adding to the bulletin board by placing inappropriate items such as toys and papers on it. For this reason, you may want to have a small bulletin board just for them to work on. A piece of poster board on the wall with small hooks on it or with Velcro fasteners will enable children to put things on their board without pins or tacks.

Since children ages 2-4 cannot read, make sure you always read everything on the bulletin board to them as you point to the words. Whenever possible, color-code the items so they can distinguish between them. Refer to each bulletin board often, asking children to remember its message. This is an excellent way to review what they have learned and to recapture their attention when it strays.

WHAT YOU NEED

Construction paper (blue, green, and a variety of other colors)
Old magazines (including some nature magazines)
Scissors
Glue
Dark colored marker
Natural items (pine cone, tree leaf, bird feather, flowers)
Small box of raisins or similar snack food
Small "touch me" music button (found in craft stores)

WHAT YOU DO

1. Enlarge the earth from the bulletin board to make a pattern. Copy it on blue paper with green for the continents. Mount the earth at the center of the bulletin board.

2. Cut letters for the caption from blue paper and mount them across the top of the board.

3. Print the "five senses" labels on rectangles of different colors of construction paper. Arrange them on the board as shown.

4. Cut out pictures from magazines for each of the categories, showing items the children can see, taste, hear, feel, and smell.

5. Ask children to choose pictures of things we see. Then help them mount their choices above by the "See It" label. Continue with taste, hear, feel, and smell.

6. Have some real items on hand for children to see, hear, taste, smell, and feel. (Let the children sample the snack food.) Then attach those items to the board.

WHAT YOU TALK ABOUT

Talk about all the wonderful things God made. Explain how we can experience them by using the five senses God gave us. Ask the children to name their favorite things to see, hear, taste, smell, and feel. Remind them that God not only made a wonderful world; He also gave us special ways to enjoy it!

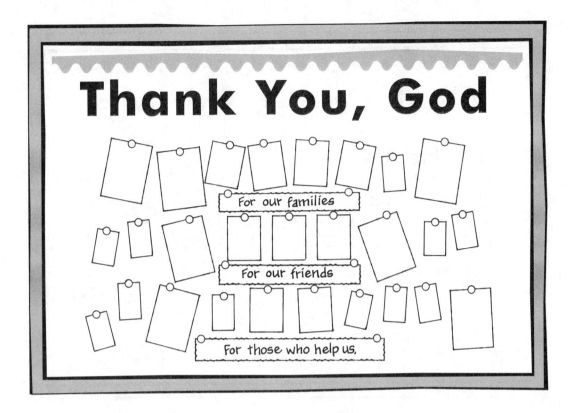

WHAT YOU NEED

Photos of children's families or paper and crayons

Construction paper (red, orange, yellow and beige or white)

Old magazines

Scissors

Dark colored marker

WHAT YOU DO

1. Cut the letters for the caption from red paper and mount them at the top of the board.

2. Print the three labels on orange, yellow and beige or white paper and attach them to the board as shown.

3. Mount each child's family picture on the board with the child's name underneath. (You may want to start on this board a few weeks in advance by taking photos of children and their families before or after class.) Otherwise, ask each child's parent to provide a photo. If you do not have photos, ask children to draw pictures of their families to attach to the board.

4. Let children draw pictures of their friends and attach them to the board.

5. Hand out old magazines and help the children find pictures of helpers, such as mail deliverer, doctor, bus driver, store clerk, teacher, etc. If possible, ask members of your church staff for photos to add to the display.

WHAT YOU TALK ABOUT

- Ask each child to describe his or her family members. Say a short prayer of thanks to God for families.
- Ask the children to explain what their friends do for them. Point out that God gives us friends to help and encourage us and He wants us to be good friends. Take a minute to say a short prayer of thanks for friends.
- Point out the many people who help us every day. Take a minute to say a short prayer of thanks for helpers.

God Cares for Me

Wherever I go,
God is there,
Caring for me,
Hearing my prayer.

At home

At church

When I'm sad

When I'm happy

When I'm sick

Night and Day

WHAT YOU NEED

Black and white construction paper
Pictures to illustrate each condition and
  place from pages 147 and 148.
Scissors
Dark colored marker
Yellow yarn

WHAT YOU DO

1 Cut the letters for the caption from black construction paper and mount them across the top of the board.

2 Print the poem on a large sheet of white paper and mount it at the top left of the board.

3 Print each label on a white paper strip.

4 Enlarge and photocopy the six illustrations. Mount each illustration on the board with the label under it.

5 Attach lengths of yarn to the poem, connecting them to the illustrations.

WHAT YOU TALK ABOUT

Read the poem to the children. Ask the children, "When does God care for you?" Talk about the different places the children spend their time and the different ways they may feel. Remind them that God is always with them no matter where they are or how they feel. Ask them to say the poem with you.

WHAT YOU NEED

Black construction paper
Scissors
White paper
Black marker
Figures of an angel, angels and shepherds,
    a manger scene, and a star from
        Christmas cards or old Sunday-school
        lessons
Christmas gift wrap and ribbon
Glue

WHAT YOU TALK ABOUT

Ask the children what the good news in each
picture is. Ask what God has given us. Ask what
we can give to God.

WHAT YOU DO

1. Cut letters for the caption from black paper and mount them on the board.

2. Glue an angel on a sheet of white paper. Print under the angel, "Good news—God is sending His Son Jesus to earth!" Mount the paper on the board. Cover it with a piece of gift-wrap and ribbon to make it look like a package. Print a number 1 on the outside.

3. Glue angels and shepherds on another sheet of white paper. Print under the picture, "Good news—God's Son has been born in a stable!" Mount the paper on the board. Cover it with a piece of gift-wrap and ribbon. Print a number 2 on the outside.

4. Glue the manger scene on a third sheet of white paper. Print under it, "Good news—Jesus came because He loves you." Mount the paper on the board, cover it with gift-wrap, and print a number 3 on the outside.

5. Glue or draw a large star on a fourth sheet of white paper. Print on the star, "Good news—you can give Jesus your love!" Mount the paper on the board, cover with gift-wrap, and print a number 4 on the outside.

6. Each week, let a child uncover one of the pictures.

WHAT YOU NEED

- Yellow construction paper
- White paper
- Picture of Jesus enlarged and copied
  from page 145
- Black marker
- Yellow and black crepe paper
- Masking tape

WHAT YOU DO

1. Print the question and answer on two pieces of yellow paper and mount them on the board as shown.

2. Mount the picture of Jesus in the middle of the board.

3. Print the cheer on white paper and mount it next to the picture of Jesus.

4. Make small pom-poms for the children by cutting strips of yellow and black crepe paper, bundling them together at one end, and taping them together for a handle.

5. After the children shake their pom-poms and say the cheer for Jesus, attach the pom-poms to the board.

WHAT YOU TALK ABOUT

- Ask the children who Jesus is. Then read the cheer to answer the question. Give each child a pom-pom to shake as they say the cheer with you. Do this several times.
- Ask the children, "Who is God's Son? Who does Jesus love?"

WHAT YOU NEED

Construction paper (black, purple, and
   lavender or pink)
Picture of Jesus and a child enlarged and
   copied from page 155
Scissors
Dark colored marker

WHAT YOU DO

1. Cut the letters for the song from purple construction paper and mount them on the board as shown.

2. Cut musical notes from black paper and scatter them over the board.

3. Mount the picture of Jesus and a child on the board.

4. Print the Bible verse, John 15:9, on lavender or pink paper and mount it on the board.

WHAT YOU TALK ABOUT

Ask the children, "Who loves you? How do you know Jesus loves you?" Sing the song together. Then read the Bible verse aloud. Remind them that we know Jesus loves us because that's what the Bible, God's Word, tells us.

**What does God want us to say
At least once every day?**

Thank You

WHAT YOU NEED

Construction paper (red, white, and
  black)
Silhouette of child praying from page
  152, enlarged and copied on black paper
Scissors
Red marker
Stapler and staples or transparent tape
Push pin or large-headed pin
Small piece of yarn

WHAT YOU DO

1. Cut letters for the caption from red construction paper and mount them on the board as shown.

2. Mount the silhouettes of children praying on both side sides of the board as shown.

3. Make a large book by folding large sheets of black paper and white paper in the middle. Staple or tape the papers together. Use the red marker to print the words THANK YOU! on the white paper inside the book.

4. Mount the closed book at the center of the board.

5. Tape or staple yarn to the front of the book. Make a small loop in the yarn and hook it over the pin you have stuck into the board next to the book. This will keep it closed when not in use.

WHAT YOU TALK ABOUT

Read the question on the bulletin board to the children. Let the children suggest answers. Open the book and read the answer—THANK YOU! Close the book again and let children take turns opening the book and reading the answer, then closing it again. Take a minute to thank God for things He has made and what He has given us.

We Are Jesus' Helpers

"We . . . are helpers." 2 Corinthians 1:24

WHAT YOU NEED

- Orange construction paper
- White paper
- Pictures to illustrate ways of helping
  (enlarge the pictures from the board or
  cut pictures from old magazines and
  story materials)
- Scissors
- Pushpins
- Brown marker

WHAT YOU DO

1. Cut the letters for the title from orange construction paper and mount them across the top of the board.

2. Cut helping hands out of orange construction paper, using the bulletin board illustration as a guide. Keep the hands, pushpins, and a marker in an envelope by the board throughout the unit.

3. Mount several pictures of helping on the board.

4. Print the Bible verse, 2 Corinthians 1:24 (KJV), on a strip of white paper and mount it across the bottom of the board.

WHAT YOU TALK ABOUT

Discuss the ways the children in the pictures are helping Jesus by helping other people. Throughout the unit, as you see a child help or hear about a way a child helped, print it on an orange helping hand and attach the hand to the bulletin board.

God Put Us Together

WHAT YOU NEED

Blue construction paper
White butcher paper (or other large
  sheet of paper)
Scissors
Pencil
Markers (black, red, and other colors)
Connecting figure pattern from page 147

WHAT YOU TALK ABOUT

Talk about the human body. Ask children to show you what their heads can do, what their arms can do, and so on. Point out that God put us together exactly the right way. Wouldn't going places be hard if God had made us with our legs attached to our heads? He made our bodies to be able to do many things—run, jump, sit, stand, walk, twirl, and even turn somersaults.

WHAT YOU DO

1 Cut the letters for the caption from blue construction paper and mount them across the top of the board.

2 Lay a large sheet of white paper on the floor and ask a child to lie down on it with arms and legs somewhat stretched out. Trace around the child's figure. Draw eyes, nose, mouth, hair, clothes, and other details on the figure. Go around the pencil outline with black marker.

3 Cut the figure into six parts: head, body, arms, and legs. Mount the body on the board. (The children will complete the figure.)

4 Use the pattern from page 147 to make several long lines of connected people. (Accordion-fold a long piece of paper, trace the figure on it, and cut it out, not cutting across the folded hands and/or feet.) Allow children to color the figures. Then mount them as a border on the board.

5 Read the caption on the bulletin board. Then give one of the paper body parts to a child. Have him or her go to the board and hold up the body part to show where it should go. Attach it for the child. Then give a part to another child. Continue until the child's figure is complete.

WHAT YOU NEED

- Blue paper
- Construction paper (white, red)
- Scissors
- Figures of preschool children from page 151, enlarged and copied
- Colored markers
- Cotton (optional)

WHAT YOU DO

1. Cover the board with blue paper.

2. Cut a large cloud shape from white paper. Print on it in large bold letters "GOD." Attach the cloud to the top of the board. Glue cotton on the cloud.

3. Color the figures of the children and mount them on the board as shown.

4. Cut small hearts from red paper and attach them to the board as shown.

5. Print the words to the rhyme in three separate parts under the children.

WHAT YOU TALK ABOUT

Have children say the words of the rhyme with you and do the actions the children on the board are doing. Ask them if they can name some things the Bible tells us to do. You may need to prompt their answers. "What does the Bible say we should do if our Mommy asks us to pick up toys?"

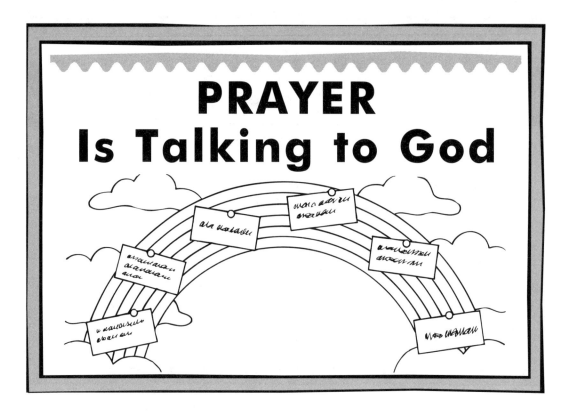

PRAYER
Is Talking to God

WHAT YOU NEED

Large white butcher paper (or gift-wrap
  with rainbows on it)
Crayons or markers
Cotton balls
Dark blue paper
Scissors
Colored index cards
Dark colored fine-tip marker

WHAT YOU DO

1. Draw a rainbow on white paper and color it (red, orange, yellow, green, blue, indigo, violet). Use the rainbow as the bulletin board background.

2. At each end of the rainbow attach a cloud shape cut from white paper.

3. Cut the letters for the caption from dark blue paper and mount them at the middle of the board.

4. Ask children to help you glue cotton balls to the clouds.

5. Ask children to name things they can say to God and things they can ask God. Print their prayers on the index cards with their names. If you have time, ask them to draw pictures on the cards, illustrating their prayers. Attach the cards to the board.

WHAT YOU TALK ABOUT

Ask the children, "What do we do when we pray?" Answer the question by reading the bulletin board caption aloud. Let the children take turns telling about their prayer cards.

WHAT YOU NEED

Red, white, and pink construction paper
Little candy hearts
Scissors
Glue
Red colored marker
Instant camera
Crayons or colored pencils

WHAT YOU DO

1. Cut the letters for the caption BE SWEET from red construction paper and mount them across the top of the board.

2. Cut a large heart from red paper and a slightly smaller one from pink paper. Use the red marker to print the Bible verse in large letters on the pink heart. Then glue the pink heart to the red one and mount it at the center of the bulletin board.

3. Cut out several smaller red, white, and pink hearts.

4. Take pictures of the children together and attach them to some of the smaller hearts. On other hearts, allow children to draw pictures of ways they have loved others. (If time is limited, have them tell about ways they have loved others and print the ways on the hearts.) Scatter the smaller hearts on the board as shown in the illustration.

5. Attach some small candy hearts to the board and give some to the children for a treat.

WHAT YOU TALK ABOUT

As the children eat candy hearts, explain that God wants us to love each other. When we love each other, we show our love by helping and being kind to each other. Read the Bible words on the large heart. Then talk about ways the children have shown their love for others.

WHAT YOU NEED

Construction paper (green, brown, red, blue, yellow)
Blue tissue paper
Scissors
Animal, fish, bird, and flower stickers
Figures of Adam and Eve from page 149

WHAT YOU DO

1. Cover the top half of the board with blue tissue paper to represent the sky. Add green paper to represent the land and blue paper to make a stream or river as shown.

2. Cut the letters for the caption from red construction paper and mount them across the top of the board.

3. Cut a large tree from green and brown paper and attach it to the board. Cut small circles from red paper to represent apples. Let children put the apples on the tree.

4. Cut a round sun from yellow paper and attach it at the top of the board.

5. Let the children choose stickers to stick on the board to show some of the wonderful things God created. Help them decide where each sticker should go.

WHAT YOU TALK ABOUT

Talk about what God created on each day of creation. Ask children to point to items you mention that are on the board. Discuss the wide variety of plants, animals, birds, and fish God made as the children place stickers on the scene. Then talk about God's creation of man and woman. Place the figures of Adam and Eve on the board. Say a short prayer of thanks for God's wonderful creation.

WHAT YOU NEED

Construction paper (white, pink, and purple)
Scissors
Black marker
Figure of a child from page 156
Pictures of family and friends (from magazines or Sunday school lessons)

WHAT YOU DO

1. Cut the letters and numbers for the caption from purple construction paper and mount them across the top of the board.

2. Attach the figure of the child to the left side of the board.

3. Print the labels with a black marker on pink paper and mount them on the right side of the board. Cut small hearts from pink and purple paper to connect each label to the child.

4. Attach pictures of family and friends beside the first two labels. Cut a cloud from white paper and print GOD on it to go beside the third label.

5. Use the black marker to print the Bible verse on a strip of purple paper and place it at the bottom of the board.

WHAT YOU TALK ABOUT

Ask the children who loves them. Give them time to answer; then read the question and answers on the board as you point to them. Talk about how our families and friends show love for us. Then explain that God showed His love for us by sending His only Son, Jesus, to earth. God loves us more than our friends love us, even more than our families love us. Then have the children say with you: "1-2-3. Who loves me? My family and friends do, but God loves me most!"

WHAT YOU NEED

Construction paper (yellow, brown)
Scissors
Brown marker
Pictures of food, water, clothes, and
    home (from magazines or enlarged
    from the board above)

WHAT YOU DO

1. Cut the letters for the caption from brown construction paper and mount them across the top of the board.

2. Cut triangles from yellow paper. Use the brown marker to print on each one "God is good." Attach the triangles to the corners of the bulletin board.

3. Allow children to choose pictures of things God gives us that we need. Help the children attach the pictures to the board.

WHAT YOU TALK ABOUT

Ask the children, "Who gives us food to eat? Clothes to wear? A place to live?" We know that God loves us because of the way He takes care of us and gives us what we need.

God's Gift to us was his Son.

WHAT YOU NEED

Black paper
Gold gift-wrap
Scissors
Illustration of Baby Jesus in the manger
   from page 150, enlarged and copied
Gold and silver star stickers
Sandpaper and straw
Glue

WHAT YOU DO

1. Cover the board with black paper for a night scene.

2. Cut the letters for the caption from gold paper and mount them across the top of the board.

3. Mount the illustration of Baby Jesus at the center of the board.

4. Cut sandpaper to fit the manger and glue it on the manger.

5. Let children stick gold and silver stars all over the black background.

6. Let children glue straw in the manger and scattered beneath the manger.

WHAT YOU TALK ABOUT

Ask the children, "What presents have you gotten for Christmas? What presents do you want for Christmas?" After they have shared for a few minutes, tell them that you know of a better gift that Someone gave them. Read the words on the board. Explain that God gave such a wonderful gift to us because He loves us. Say a brief prayer of thanks for God's great gift.

Jesus Grew Just Like You

WHAT YOU NEED

- Green construction paper
- Tan or brown paper (package wrap will work well)
- Scissors
- Black fine-tip marker
- Figure of Jesus in the manger from page 150

WHAT YOU DO

1. Cover the bulletin board with tan or brown paper on which you have drawn inch and foot marks. Number the bottom mark "2 feet" and continue up the board.

2. Cut the letters for the caption from green construction paper and mount them across the bottom of the board.

3. Enlarge and copy the figure of Jesus as a baby. Use the illustration to guide you to draw figures of Jesus as he grew as a child. Mount the figures on the board as shown.

4. Measure each child's height and record it at the proper place by the inch marks on the side of the board.

WHAT YOU TALK ABOUT

Talk about how much the children have grown. Point out the figure of Jesus in the manger. Ask the children if Jesus stayed a small baby. Point out the growth of Jesus as shown by the three figures on the board. Read the caption. Talk about some of the ways Jesus' growing up years were like those of the children. (He had to learn how to walk and talk, He outgrew His clothes, He skinned His knees, He went to school, and so on.)

WHAT YOU NEED

Construction paper (black and yellow)
Scissors
Black marker
Figure of Jesus from page 144, enlarged
   and copied
Crayons, colored pencils, or markers
Illustrations enlarged from the board

WHAT YOU DO

1. Cut the letters for the caption from black construction paper and mount them across the top and bottom of the bulletin board.

2. Mount the figure of Jesus at the center of the board.

3. Print the five labels with a black marker on yellow paper and mount them on the board as shown.

4. Allow the children to color the illustrations of things Jesus can do. Then read each label to the children and ask them to find the picture that goes with the label and help you mount it on the board.

WHAT YOU TALK ABOUT

Ask the children to tell about some of the wonderful things Jesus did. Ask, "Why can Jesus do such wonderful things?" Jesus can do these things because He is God's Son.

My Best Friend Is Jesus

WHAT YOU NEED

- Construction paper (yellow, green, and brown)
- Scissors
- Small photo of each child
- Picture of Jesus from page 145
- Pictures of flowers (from a gardening catalog or magazine)

WHAT YOU DO

1. Cut the letters for the caption from green construction paper and mount them across the top and bottom of the board.

2. Cut a large circle from brown paper and attach it to the center of the board. Attach the picture of Jesus to the paper.

3. Cut a flower petal shape from yellow paper for each child.

4. Give each child a flower petal and help him attach his photo to the petal. If you do not have photos, have children draw pictures of themselves.

5. Help children attach the petals on the board around the center of the flower. (If you have a large number of children, make more than one flower.)

6. Let children choose pictures of flowers and help them scatter the pictures all over the board.

WHAT YOU TALK ABOUT

Ask children to tell you about their friends. Then draw their attention to the bulletin board and read the caption. Explain that we like to spend time with our friends and talk to them. Jesus is our best friend. He wants to be close to us. He wants us to talk to Him. He wants to help us. We will never have a better friend than Jesus.

Look inside to find out who Jesus loves.

WHAT YOU NEED

Construction paper (orange and brown)
Cardboard
Mirror (between 4" x 6" and 9" x 12")
Black marker
Brown yarn
Stapler and staples or tape
Push pin

WHAT YOU DO

1. Use the black marker to print the instructions on the orange paper. Mount it on the left side of the board.

2. Make a cardboard frame for the mirror and attach it to the right side of the board.

3. Make a door from brown construction paper to cover the mirror. Attach the door to the board only on one side so it can be opened from the other side.

4. Staple or tape a piece of brown yarn to the door. Make a loop in the yarn and hook it over a pushpin or big-headed pin next to the door to keep it closed.

WHAT YOU TALK ABOUT

Read the caption on the bulletin board. Choose a child to open the door and look inside. (The child will see his or her own reflection.) Let each child have a turn. Point out to the children that they don't ever have to be afraid because Jesus is with them. No matter what happens to them, Jesus is there.

WHAT YOU NEED
Red construction paper
Scissors
Pictures of the Good Samaritan, Timothy, Peter, and Paul (enlarged from the board above or from Sunday school lessons)
Black marker
Small shoebox covered with gift-wrap
3" x 5" colored index cards (cut in half)

WHAT YOU TALK ABOUT
Remind children that Jesus wants them all to be good helpers. Talk about some of the ways they can help at Sunday school and at home. Talk about the Bible people on the board. Discuss what each one did to be a good helper for Jesus. Then read the caption on the board and the instructions. Let the children take turns drawing cards from the helper's box.

WHAT YOU DO

1. Cut the letters for the caption from red construction paper and mount them at the top of the board.

2. Mount the pictures of the four Bible people on the board as shown.

3. Use the black marker to print the instructions on red paper. Mount it near the bottom of the board.

4. Print on the side of the box "Helper's Box." Attach it to the board beneath the instructions.

5. Draw simple sketches on the colored cards to show ways of helping. (Examples: picking up toys, brushing teeth, obeying cheerfully, caring for pets, and so on.) Use simple stick-figure symbols on the cards, such as a hand on a toy, a toothbrush, a happy face, and a goldfish in a bowl. Also print the helping activity on each card so the child's parents can read it and remind the child how to help.

6. Place the cards in the box for children to draw out and take home.
   NOTE: If you use this board for several weeks, make new helper cards for each week.

We Love God

We pray

We read the Bible

We obey

We sing to God

WHAT YOU NEED

Construction paper (a variety of colors)
Scissors
Black marker
Bible, praying hands, music, and happy child symbols (enlarged from the board)
Fun stickers

WHAT YOU DO

1. Print the title "We Love God" on a large strip of paper and attach it at the top of the board.

2. Use the black marker to print the instructions on four different colors of construction paper strips. Attach them to the board as shown.

3. Attach the appropriate symbol to the board beside each instruction.

4. Each time during the weeks of the unit that a child reads or listens to the Bible, prays, sings to God, or obeys, allow him to attach a fun sticker to the appropriate place on the bulletin board.

WHAT YOU TALK ABOUT

- Discuss each way to love God. Remind children that even though they can't read the Bible, they can learn from God's Word by paying attention in Sunday School and listening to what their parents teach them about the Bible.
- Ask children what we can talk to God about. What can we tell Him? What can we ask Him?
- Talk about singing praise to God. We do that at church, but we can also do it at home or wherever we are. Take a minute to sing together a simple chorus such as "God Is So Good."
- Finally talk about obeying. Ask the children to look at the face on the board. Is the face happy or sad? The happy face shows us that God wants us to obey cheerfully, without fussing or complaining. When parents tell us to do something, God wants us to do it and not argue or cry or pout. If we do all these things, we'll show God, and other people, how much we love Him.

GOD SAYS

Don't be selfish   Always share

WHAT YOU NEED

Construction paper (black, red, and white)
Scissors
Black marker
Illustrations of selfishness and sharing from page 148

WHAT YOU DO

1. Cut the letters for the caption from red construction paper and mount them at the top of the board.

2. Cut two large circles from black paper and two slightly smaller circles from white paper. Mount the white circles on the board on top of the black circles, leaving a black border, to look like traffic signs.

3. Attach the two illustrations to the circular signs.

4. Cut a strip of red paper and attach it across the selfishness sign like a slash.

5. Use the black marker to print the labels on white paper. Mount them on the board beneath the signs.

WHAT YOU TALK ABOUT

Ask the children to name things they can share with friends and with family. Ask them to tell something they will share this week.

WHAT YOU NEED

Gold and silver paper
White paper
Star pattern from page 144
Scissors
Black marker
Star stickers
Photo of each child
Clear tape

WHAT YOU DO

1. Print the questions on strips of white paper and mount them at the top and bottom of the board. Add some star stickers around the words.

2. Using the pattern, cut several stars from gold and silver paper. Mount the stars on the board.

3. When a child helps out in class in some way, tape his or her photo to a star and write on the star the name of the child and the helpful deed done. If you do not have photos, simply write the name and the helpful act on the star.

4. Find reasons to "star" all the children on the board.

WHAT YOU TALK ABOUT

Talk about all the things we can do to be helpful. Ask the children to suggest ways they can help at church (handing out papers, picking up litter, being quiet, praying, doing what the teacher says, and so on). Draw their attention to the bulletin board. Tell them that all helpers will get to be on the stars for everyone to see. You may want to limit the stars to two or three a week.

Bulletin boards are excellent tools for focusing children's attention. Every classroom should have at least one bulletin board that is changed frequently to correlate with what the children are learning. The bulletin boards on the following pages introduce and illustrate important truths from God's Word. Many of them involve children in a variety of ways—drawing and cutting out pictures, writing down or drawing their thoughts and responses to what they learn, even singing. You may also want to let your children help with cutting out letters and word cards and mounting them on the board.

To reinforce the impact of the bulletin boards and help children remember them, provide a small take-home item related to the board when possible. (For example, let each child make a small paper chain to take home as a reminder that God never breaks a promise as illustrated in the bulletin board with the large paper chain on page 35.)

Use the bulletin board to help children review a lesson or unit of study or refer to it when you see that their attention is beginning to stray. Often a visual on which a child can focus her attention helps her concentrate on the lesson.

If you don't have a permanent bulletin board in your room, cover a large piece of cardboard with fabric or paper for a homemade bulletin board or mount the words and pictures on a large sheet of poster board that you can take home and bring back each week.

WHAT YOU NEED

Saucer-sized circles cut from construction paper (in a variety of colors)

Large circle cut from blue paper

Black marker

Pencils and crayons or colored markers

WHAT YOU DO

1 Print in large letters on the large circle "Praise the Maker of It All" and mount the circle at the center of the bulletin board.

2 Hand out circles, pencils, and crayons or colored markers to the children. Have them draw on the circles some of the things God created: sun, moon, trees, animals, flowers, people, and so on.

3 Let the children mount their Creation circles on the board around the big circle. You may want to let each child put more than one Creation circle on the board, depending on the number of children you have and the size of the board.

WHAT YOU TALK ABOUT

Discuss each drawing, asking the children to say on what day of Creation that particular thing was made. Then ask the children what else God created that is not shown on the board. When everyone has had an opportunity to share, remind them that everything in the world, in the universe and beyond, was made by one Creator—God. Take a minute to pray together, encouraging each child to thank God for one of the things He created.

God Never Broke a Promise and He Never Will!

WHAT YOU NEED

Red construction paper
Scissors
Construction paper cut into strips
  (a variety of colors)
Glue or clear tape
Dark colored markers

WHAT YOU TALK ABOUT

Review the promises God made to Noah, Abraham, Isaac, Jacob and others. Discuss how God kept each promise. Ask the children if they know some promises God has made to us. To get them started, you may want to read some Bible verses with promises in them, such as Acts 16:31; Matthew 7:7; John 14:2, 3. Ask them if God has kept all the promises He made to us. Point out that some of them have not happened yet, such as His promise to come back someday and take us to heaven with Him. But just as He has always kept His promises to those who love Him, He will continue to do so.

WHAT YOU DO

1. Cut letters for the caption, top and bottom, from red paper and mount them on the board as shown.

2. Give each child two or three strips of paper and a marker. Talk about some of the promises God made to Bible people you have studied, such as Noah, Abraham, Isaac, and Jacob. Assign each child a different promise to write on a strip of paper. (Have an adult helper or older child write for younger children.)

3. Have one child tape or glue one of the promise strips together at the ends to make a loop (with the promise on the outside). Have a second child connect a promise strip through the first child's loop and glue or tape the ends together. Continue until all the promise strips are connected together in a paper chain.

4. Mount the promise chain across the board as shown. If the chain is very long, you may want to attach it in the middle as well as on the ends.
OPTION: Cut smaller strips of paper and let children make their own promise chains to take home to remind them of God's promises. They could draw pictures of some of the promises mentioned in the Bible verses listed in *What You Talk About*.

God takes care of us each day.

He provides, protects, and shows the way.

WHAT YOU NEED

Blue paper
Construction paper (brown and light
   colors)
Scissors
Velcro
Dark blue and black markers
Glue
Doll pattern on page 146

WHAT YOU TALK ABOUT

Read the rhyming caption on the board and talk about how God cared for the Israelites. Then ask the children to share some of the ways God cares for us each day.

WHAT YOU DO

1. Print the rhyming caption on two long strips of light colored construction paper and mount them at the top and bottom of the board.

2. Cut two large pieces of blue paper to cover most of the board. Use a marker to draw wavy lines on the paper to make it look like water. Mount the two pieces on the board as shown and fold them back from the center.

3. Cut a piece of brown paper to fit between the two pieces of folded back blue paper. Use a black marker to make small marks on the brown paper to look like stones. Mount the brown paper on the board between the two pieces of blue paper.

4. Glue small pieces of Velcro to the two folded back pieces of blue paper to hold them together when they're closed.

5. Copy the paper doll pattern on page 146 and give one to each child to color and draw on features and clothing.

6. As you talk about how God opened a path in the sea for His people to cross over, fold back the "sea" on the board and let the children walk their people across the water on the path.

WHAT YOU NEED

Gold or silver wrapping paper
Black paper
Scissors
Wise men figures cut from Christmas
   cards or old Sunday school lessons
Figure of Jesus from page 144
Photos or self portraits of the children

WHAT YOU DO

1. Cover the board with black paper.

2. Cut a large star from gold or silver paper and mount it on the left side of the board. Mount wise men figures under the star.

3. Attach the figure of Jesus on the right side of the board. Mount photos or self portraits of the children under or around Jesus.

4. Cut letters for the caption from gold or silver paper and mount them on the board. (Or use a black marker to print the caption on a strip of white paper.)

WHAT YOU TALK ABOUT

Ask children what the wise men gave Jesus. Ask them to name some things they can give to Jesus, such as love, worship and thanks, obedience.

WHAT YOU NEED

Orange construction paper

Scissors

Figure of Jesus from page 144, enlarged and copied

Strip of white paper

Black marker

Small photos of children or group photo

WHAT YOU DO

1 Cut letters for the Bible verse caption from orange construction paper and mount them on the bulletin board as shown.

2 Mount the figure of Jesus on the left side of the board.

3 On the white strip of paper print "We will obey and be friends of Jesus." Let each child who wants to, sign the strip. Mount it under the Bible verse.

4 Mount the photos of the children or the group photo under the white paper strip.

WHAT YOU TALK ABOUT

Ask a volunteer to read the Bible verse on the board. Discuss what it means. Ask the children if they want to be Jesus' friends. Discuss when it is easy and when it is hard to obey His commands. Ask those who want to obey Jesus to sign their names on the white paper strip. Each week refer to the bulletin board and ask children if they have been obeying the Lord's commands. Let them share ways they have done this.

Reach Out to Others as Jesus Did

WHAT YOU NEED
Construction paper (white, brown, pink)
Scissors
Pencils
Black markers

WHAT YOU DO

1 Cut the letters for the caption from brown paper and mount them in the center of the board as shown.

2 Hand out pencils, scissors, and construction paper. Let the children trace around their hands (slightly open) and cut them out separately. (You'll need to help younger children with the cutting.)

3 Have the children print or draw on their hands some practical ways to reach out to others as Jesus did. (Examples: Visit someone who is sick, rake the neighbor's yard, invite a schoolmate to church, be friendly.)

4 Mount the hands, touching one another, around the bulletin board.

WHAT YOU TALK ABOUT
Ask children to share the ways they will reach out to others. Each week, have children point to the hands that show ways they have loved or helped others that week.

WHAT YOU NEED

Construction paper (dark blue, light blue, and white)

Scissors

Figure of Jesus from page 144, enlarged and copied

Black marker

Glue

WHAT YOU DO

1. Cut letters for the caption from dark blue paper and mount them on the board.

2. Mount the top half of the figure of Jesus at the center of the board.

3. Draw the simple sketches from the board on white paper. Allow children to color the sketches and glue them to light blue paper.

4. Give clues about each story shown in the sketches and have children choose the correct sketch. Print the label under the sketch when it is guessed correctly and mount it on the board. Possible clues: Before this person met Jesus, he had never heard a thunderstorm or heard a bird sing. This person had never seen the sun or another person's face before he met Jesus. This man couldn't hold anything in his hands or reach out and touch another person before he met Jesus. This girl was so sick that she died, and then she met Jesus. Jesus' disciples were scared of this terrible storm before Jesus woke up.

WHAT YOU TALK ABOUT

Ask the children, "Can anyone else do the things Jesus did? Why could Jesus make a blind man see? Make a deaf man hear? Make a little girl live again? Make a storm stop? Heal a man's hand?" Explain that only Jesus could do these things because He is the Son of God. Ask children to tell about other wonderful things Jesus did!

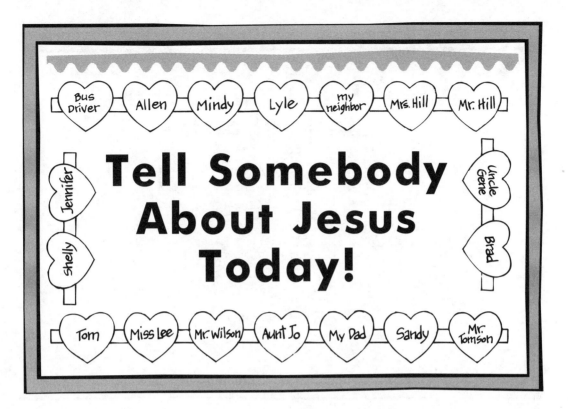

WHAT YOU NEED

Black construction paper
Several long strips of red or pink paper
Scissors
Black marker

WHAT YOU DO

1. Cut letters for the caption from black construction paper and mount them at the center of the board.

2. Accordion fold a strip of paper and draw a heart on it with connecting tabs on each side (touching the folds).

3. Cut out the heart without cutting across either fold. Unfold the paper and you'll have several connected hearts. Make enough to go all the way around your bulletin board.

4. Mount the hearts around the board as shown.

5. Ask the children to think about some people that they want to tell about Jesus. (Let each child name two or three people, depending on how many children you have.) Print the names of the people on the hearts on the bulletin board.

WHAT YOU TALK ABOUT

Ask volunteers to share what they would say to someone who didn't know Jesus. Remind children that everyone can tell somebody about Jesus; we don't have to be a certain age or size or have a certain job. Anyone who knows and loves Jesus can tell other people about Him. Encourage the children to talk to the people whose names are on the hearts to share Jesus with them. Each week ask the children if they have told others about Jesus. Allow time for them to share what they told and who they told about Jesus.

When hard times come, talk about

GOD'S SON

WHAT YOU NEED

Black paper
Yellow construction paper
Shiny gold wrapping paper
Scissors

WHAT YOU DO

1. Cover the bulletin board with black paper.

2. Cut letters for the caption, all except the words "GOD'S SON" from yellow paper and mount them on the board as shown.

3. Cut a large sun from gold wrapping paper and mount it on the board.

4. Cut the letters for "GOD'S SON" from black paper and attach them to the sun.
OPTION: Provide black and yellow construction paper, white crayons or chalk, scissors, glue, and pencils. Cut suns out of the yellow construction paper. Discuss hard times the children have, such as times they are afraid or sad. Ask them to draw hard times on the paper. Then help them glue yellow suns on the paper and write or draw a picture of what they can remember about Jesus during that time. Suggestions: He loves me. He always takes care of me. He is always with me.

WHAT YOU TALK ABOUT

Discuss some specific instances when we can talk about Jesus in hard times (when we are sick we can tell our visitors how much Jesus helps us, when something sad happens in our family we can tell those around us that Jesus gives us comfort).

WHAT YOU NEED
- White paper
- Brown paper (such as package wrap)
- Scissors
- Black marker
- Small brad fastener
- Donkey and legs pattern from page 151

WHAT YOU DO

1. Print the caption on a large piece of white paper and mount it on the board as shown.

2. Enlarge the donkey pattern on page 151 on brown paper, going over the details with a black marker.

3. Cut out the donkey, cutting out his hind legs separately. Fasten the legs to the donkey with a small brad fastener so the legs can be moved as if the donkey is kicking.

4. Mount the donkey on the board as shown. Let the children move the donkey's leg as you read the caption.
OPTION: Provide white paper, smaller donkeys and legs cut from brown paper, brads, glue, and pencils. Help children make their own "do right" pictures by gluing the donkey to paper. Help them fasten the donkey's leg with a brad. Then ask them to share times they have done right. Have them print the times on their pictures, or print for them if they are unable.

WHAT YOU TALK ABOUT
Ask the children if they ever fuss or complain when they're told to do something. Explain that when a donkey doesn't want to do something, he doesn't fuss like we do. He kicks and hee-haws! (Move the donkey's leg as you say this.) Sometimes we act like stubborn donkeys, kicking up a fuss when we should be obeying instead. God wants us to do the right thing, obeying our parents and doing what the Bible teaches.

Follow His Footsteps

WHAT YOU NEED

Construction paper (red, brown, tan, and white)

Scissors

Black marker

Figures of child and Jesus from pages 151 and 152, enlarged and copied

WHAT YOU DO

1. Cut letters for the caption from red paper and mount them on the board.

2. Cut a path from brown paper and mount it on the board.

3. Color the figures of the child and Jesus and mount them where shown on the board.

4. Cut footprints from tan paper. Print a phrase of the Bible verse on each footprint. Attach them to the path as shown. OPTION: Make extra footprints for the children. Each week allow children to print a way they followed Jesus and attach their footprints to the board.

WHAT YOU TALK ABOUT

Ask children to say the verse with you. Ask what it means to follow Jesus' footsteps. Have children name ways they can follow Jesus.

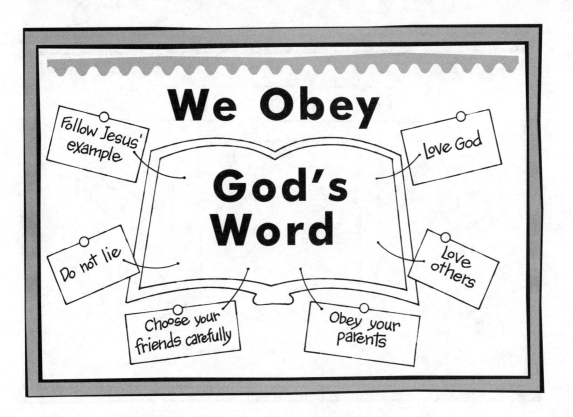

WHAT YOU NEED

Construction paper (black, white, and yellow)
Scissors
Glue
Black marker
Black or yellow yarn

WHAT YOU DO

1. Cut letters for the caption from black paper and mount them at the top of the board.

2. Cut a large open Bible shape from black paper and a slightly smaller one from white paper. Glue the white shape to the black one to look like an open Bible.

3. Cut letters for "GOD'S WORD" from black paper and glue them on the open Bible. Mount the Bible at the center of the board.

4. Cut several word cards from yellow paper. Ask children to name some things the Bible teaches us. Choose several of their suggestions to print on the yellow cards.

5. Mount the yellow cards around the board and attach yarn to connect the Bible with each word card.

WHAT YOU TALK ABOUT

Talk about the importance of studying God's Word to find out what God wants us to do, then obeying it. Ask children to call out some Bible verses they have learned. Discuss how to obey what the verses say. If you wish, discuss how the children have obeyed each week and add yellow cards telling how they obeyed God's Word that week.

WHAT YOU NEED

Long strip of pink paper
Construction paper (pink, light brown,
    and tan)
Scissors
Black markers
Figure of a child praying from page 152,
    or the child from the board above,
    enlarged and copied

WHAT YOU DO

1. Print the caption on a long strip of pink paper and mount it across the top of the board.

2. Mount the figure of a child praying at the center of the board.

3. Hand out pink, brown, and tan construction paper to the children as well as black markers and scissors to older children. Help the children trace around their hands (fingers together) to look like praying hands and cut them out.

4. Let children share ways God has helped them. You may need to give them suggestions, such as a time He helped when they were afraid or sad, or how He has helped by giving them families and friends. Write each child's thank-You prayer to God for that help on the hand. (Older children may do this for themselves.)

5. Let the children mount their hand-shaped prayers on the board.

WHAT YOU TALK ABOUT

Explain that God wants to hear from us often, not just when we have problems or needs, but also when things are going right. After the children have worded their prayers and mounted them on the board, take a few minutes to let each one thank God out loud for His help.

I will praise you, O Lord, with all my heart; I will tell of all

YOUR WONDERS.

Psalm 9:1

WHAT YOU NEED

Construction paper (a variety of colors)
White paper
Figures of Elijah and Elisha from page 149
Scissors
Dark colored marker
Crayons or colored markers

WHAT YOU TALK ABOUT

Ask a child to read the Bible verse from the board. Explain that God gave both Elijah and Elisha the power to do miracles. Discuss the miracles pictured. Then ask, "Why don't we praise Elijah and Elisha for doing these wonderful things?" Remind the children that it was God who did the miracles through these two men. He is the one who deserves our praise. And He wants us to tell other people about His power and love.

WHAT YOU DO

1 Print the first part of the Bible verse on a long strip of white paper and mount it at the top of the board.

2 Cut the letters for "YOUR WONDERS" out of different colors of bright construction paper and mount them in the center of the board. Print "Psalm 9:1" on a small slip of paper and attach it below the letters.

3 Attach the figure of Elijah on the left side of the board and the figure of Elisha on the right.

4 Hand out white paper and crayons or markers. Have the children draw pictures of some of the miracles performed by Elijah and Elisha. For Elijah, they could draw ravens bringing food, the oil and flour not running out, and fire coming down on the altar. For Elisha, they could draw Naaman coming out of the water, and the Shunammite woman's son coming back to life.

5 When the children's pictures are done, mount them on colored construction paper and attach them to the board.

WHAT YOU NEED

Construction paper (purple, black, and white)
Scissors
Black marker
Small photos of children (optional)

WHAT YOU DO

1. Cut letters for the caption from purple paper and mount them at the top of the board.

2. Print the words of the song on a large sheet of white paper and mount it at the center of the board.

3. Cut large musical notes from black paper. Ask the children to tell about times when God has answered prayers. As they share, print their names on white paper circles and attach them to the musical notes or attach their photos to the notes. Help each child mount his note on the board.

4. Thank God for answering prayers by singing the song to the tune of "I Will Make You Fishers of Men."

WHAT YOU TALK ABOUT

Each week, ask children to share ways God has answered prayers. Encourage them to tell their friends and family what God has done for them. Sing a second verse to the song:

"Thank the Lord and tell everyone, tell everyone, tell everyone.
Thank the Lord and tell everyone that He answers prayer.
That He answers prayer, that He answers prayer.
Thank the Lord and tell everyone that He answers prayer."

WHAT YOU NEED
Birthday gift-wrap
Construction paper (white, red, and
    green)
Scissors
Colored markers
Colored string or ribbon
Birthday candles
Glue
Balloons (optional)

WHAT YOU DO

1 Cover the bulletin board with birthday gift-wrap.

2 Cut letters for the caption from red or green paper (whichever shows up best on the gift-wrap background) and mount them on the board as shown.

3 Enlarge the figure of the cake on white paper or draw your own and color it. Mount it at the center of the board.

4 Glue real birthday candles to the top of the cake.

5 Cut large circles from construction paper to look like balloons or blow up real balloons.

6 Ask children to share what they want to say to Jesus on His birthday. Print their birthday wishes for Jesus on the balloons, attach strings to them, and help them mount the balloons on the board.

WHAT YOU TALK ABOUT
Ask the children how they like to celebrate their birthdays. Point out that we treat people special on their birthdays and try to give them the presents they want. Ask the children what they think Jesus would like to have for a birthday gift. Sing happy birthday to Jesus, then let each child express a special birthday wish to Jesus or say what he or she wants to give Jesus.

WHAT YOU NEED

Light colored construction paper
Dark colored markers
Figure of Jesus from page 144, enlarged
and copied
Scissors

WHAT YOU DO

1. Mount the figure of Jesus at the center of the board.

2. Print the question and answer on separate sheets of construction paper and mount them on the board as shown.

3. Ask children to think of some of the names of Jesus. Print the names of Jesus on word cards made from colored construction paper. Allow children to decorate the cards by coloring with markers or by cutting borders. Help the children mount the cards on the board.

WHAT YOU TALK ABOUT

Ask children what names someone might give to describe them or what they do. (Student, son or daughter, sister or brother, helper, friend, and so on.) Ask them what they think is the best name for Jesus. Say a prayer of praise, using the different names of Jesus.

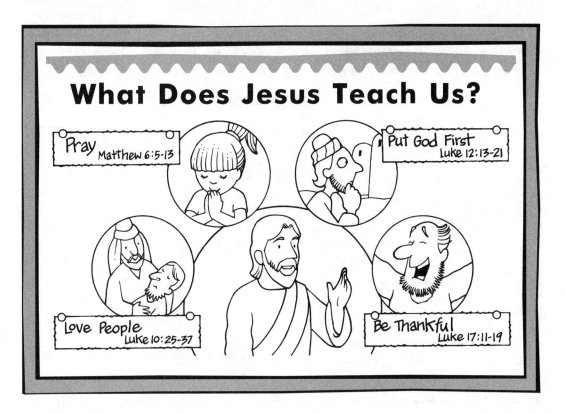

WHAT YOU NEED

- Construction paper (green and a variety of other colors)
- Scissors
- Black marker
- Figure of Jesus from page 145
- Bible story illustrations (from Sunday school lessons or enlarged from board)

WHAT YOU DO

1. Cut letters for the caption from green paper and mount them at the top of the board.

2. Mount the figure of Jesus in the center of the board.

3. Print the four things Jesus taught and the Bible references on colored strips of paper and mount them on the board as shown.

4. Read the strips telling what Jesus taught. Then show children the Bible story pictures and have them tell about the story and choose which picture goes with each strip. Let them help you attach the pictures to the board next to the strips.

WHAT YOU TALK ABOUT

As you study the Bible story each week, refer to the board and ask children to share ways they can pray like Jesus taught us, put God first unlike the rich farmer, love people like the Good Samaritan, and be thankful like the leper.

Jesus is special because . . .

WHAT YOU NEED
Construction paper (a variety of colors)
Scissors
Crayons or colored markers
Tracing shapes cut from poster board
(triangle, circle, rectangle, square)

WHAT YOU DO

1. Cut letters for the caption from several different dark colors of paper and mount them on the board.

2. Hand out paper, scissors, and crayons or markers to the children. Have each child trace two copies of a geometric shape onto colored paper and cut out the shapes. (If you have younger children in your class, cut out the shapes ahead of time.)

3. Talk about ways Jesus is special. Be sure to include the stories listed on the board. Print or have the children print one of the ways Jesus is special on each of their shapes. On the matching shapes, the children should draw pictures of the way Jesus is special. Print each child's name on her picture.

4. Put the two shapes together with the picture on top. Let the children help you mount the shapes on the board. Leave the top shapes free at the bottom so that you can lift them up and read the messages underneath.

WHAT YOU TALK ABOUT
Discuss the Bible stories illustrated on the board (Jesus walking on water, the feeding of the 5,000, raising the widow's son, healing the lame man at the pool, and healing the official's son) and others which demonstrate Jesus' special powers and shows His love for people. Ask children to share other reasons they know Jesus is special.

WHAT YOU NEED

- Shiny paper (blue and gold)
- Construction paper (gray or brown and a variety of colors)
- Scissors
- Figure of Jesus from page 144, copied and enlarged
- Cardboard
- Crayons or colored markers
- Glue

WHAT YOU DO

1. Cover the board with shiny blue paper.

2. Cut letters for the caption from shiny gold paper and mount them on the board.

3. Cut the tomb and stone from gray or brown paper and attach them to the board.

4. Accordion-fold a strip of cardboard and glue it on the back of the figure of Jesus. Attach the other end of the cardboard spring to the center of the board so that the figure of Jesus stands out from the board.

5. Hand out construction paper, scissors, glue, and crayons or colored markers and let the children create spring flowers of all kinds.

6. Mount the flowers on the board as shown.

WHAT YOU TALK ABOUT

Ask volunteers to explain what happened to Jesus after He died on the cross. Explain that we celebrate Easter because Jesus came back to life after He died. The word we use to describe His coming back to life is "Resurrection." Ask the children if they know where flowers spend the cold winter. Explain that they die back in the fall and then come back to life in the spring. These spring flowers remind us of new life—Jesus' new life after His death and the new life He promises those who believe in Him. This is a wonderful message that we should be telling everyone—not just at Easter, but all the time.

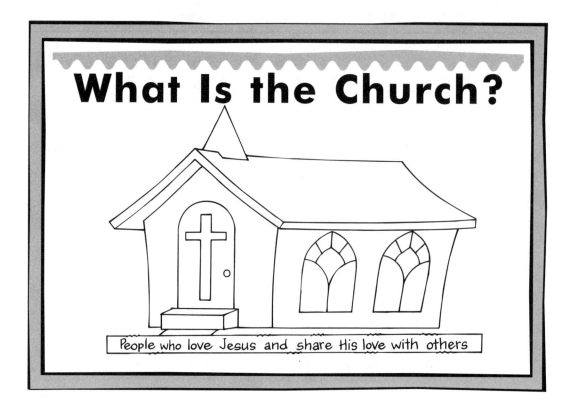

What Is the Church?

People who love Jesus and share His love with others

WHAT YOU NEED

Blue construction paper
White poster board
White paper
Magazines
Scissors
Crayons or colored markers
Glue

WHAT YOU TALK ABOUT

Read the question on the board and let children share their ideas about what God's church is. Explain that the church is not a building. Rather, it is people who believe in Jesus. Ask a volunteer to read the answer on the board. Explain that the church is made up of Christians in Africa, Asia, Russia, America, Canada—people from all over the world. We meet in different places and we may speak different languages and worship in different ways, but all that believe in Jesus belong to God's church. Let children take turns opening the windows and doors of the church to see the people inside.

WHAT YOU DO

1 Cut letters for the caption from blue paper and mount them at the top of the board. Print the answer to the question on a strip of blue paper and mount it at the bottom of the board.

2 Draw a large church building on white poster board and cut it out. Cut three sides of the windows and doors of the church, so that they can be folded back.

3 Glue the church to the bulletin board, leaving the cut-out windows and doors free.

4 Hand out magazines and scissors. Have the children look for and cut out figures of people of all kinds, colors, sizes, and ages. Help children glue the figures of people inside the windows and doors of the church.

5 When the glue has dried, fold closed the windows and doors. You may need to hold them closed with pushpins.

6 To answer the question on the board, open the windows and doors of the church.

WHAT YOU NEED

Construction paper (black and white
    or yellow)
Scissors
Colored markers (including black)
Pages from a variety of old calendars

WHAT YOU DO

1. Cut words for the caption from black paper and mount them on the board.

2. Draw a calendar for the current month on white or yellow paper and attach it to the board.

3. Print the Bible verse on a strip of paper and attach it to the bottom of the board.

4. Mount pages from old calendars next to the new one.

5. Ask children to tell some right things they can do every day. Print their suggestions on different days of the calendar. Older children can print themselves.
OPTION: If you will be using the board throughout the unit, let children share what they have done right each week. Print each child's name and what she did right on that week's space on the calendar.

WHAT YOU TALK ABOUT

Ask, "When is the right time to do the right thing?" Explain that God expects us to do right every day—all the time. Ask children to share right things they can do when they get up in the morning, when they eat lunch, when they play with their family and friends, when they go to bed.

WHAT YOU NEED

Construction paper (red and pink)
Scissors
Brown or gray fuzzy fabric (such as flannel or corduroy)
Craft eyes or buttons for eyes
Glue
Black marker

WHAT YOU DO

1 Cut letters for the caption from red paper and glue them to a pink circle for a talk balloon. Attach the circle to the board as shown with little pink circles connecting it to the bear.

2 Enlarge the teddy bear shape and use it as a pattern to cut a large bear from fabric.

3 Glue craft eyes or buttons to the bear's face, draw a nose, and attach the bear to the board.

4 Print the Bible verse and prayer on separate sheets of pink paper and mount them on the board next to the bear.

WHAT YOU TALK ABOUT

Draw children's attention to the bear. Ask them if they ever say something and then put their hands over their mouths wishing they hadn't said it. Have they had people say things to them that hurt? Ask a volunteer to read the caption. Read the Bible verse. Explain that if we ask God to help us, He will set a guard over our mouths and help us say helpful, encouraging, and honest words instead of hateful, foolish words. Ask a volunteer to read the prayer on the board. Ask the children to bow their heads and pray that prayer to God.

WHAT YOU NEED

Construction paper (red, green, yellow,
   and white or brown)
Scissors
Black marker
Two large craft sticks
Fabric (for clothing)
Glue

WHAT YOU DO

1. Enlarge the figure of the child from the illustration above and cut her out. Use the fabric to cut out clothes that a school crossing guard would wear. Glue the clothes on the figure of the child and attach the figure to the board.

2. Make a round sign from green paper and print on it GO DO RIGHT. Make an octagonal sign from red paper and print on it STOP DOING WRONG.

3. Glue each sign to a craft stick and mount it on the board with the handle in the child's hand.

4. Cut yellow strips of paper to make the crossing. Have children print on the strips of paper ways that they will start doing right. Attach the strips to the board to make the crossing as shown in the illustration.

WHAT YOU TALK ABOUT

If the children do not know what a crossing guard is, explain it to them. Then ask them what the crossing guard on the board is telling them. Explain that God's Word, like a crossing guard, helps us see the right thing to do and keeps us from doing wrong if we obey it. Ask the children to share some examples of right and wrong decisions they are faced with every day. Discuss what the Bible teaches about these. Remind them that the crossing guard is there for our protection. If we disobey or ignore him, we could be in danger! How could disobeying the Bible be dangerous?

Bulletin Boards for Ages 8-10

Bulletin boards are an ideal way to illustrate Bible stories, Bible truths, and important concepts. They can be used to grab students' attention, to emphasize the most important points in a lesson, to give children opportunity to express their ideas or feelings, and to review facts and events.

Children obviously learn by doing. Consequently, many of the bulletin boards on the following 24 pages encourage student participation. Let your students help as much as possible with each bulletin board. Some will want to come early to class to help you. Other early arrivers may need the discipline of concentrating on something worthwhile until class begins. Assign bulletin board tasks that make the most of your students' gifts and abilities. Some children may not be good at drawing, but are able to cut out paper letters evenly and neatly. Other children may be especially good at organizing and arranging where things should go on the bulletin board.

Making class bulletin boards provides excellent opportunities for children to work together and learn to cooperate. Encourage harmony, not competition. They will enjoy learning to work peaceably together and the result will be something they can proudly show their parents and friends.

Use these bulletin boards, and the preparation of them, as springboards to discussion and the sharing of ideas. Encourage students to ask questions when they don't understand something. Whenever possible, help them look up answers in their Bibles for themselves rather than just telling them the answers.

To let the bulletin boards have even more impact, give each student a small notebook. Every time you put together a new bulletin board, have the children draw a sketch of it in their notebooks. You may want to keep the notebooks until the end of the quarter or the year; then let the children take them home to share with their families some of the lessons they have learned.

WHAT YOU NEED

Shiny/slick coated white paper
Pencils and paints or colored markers
Purple construction paper
Scissors

WHAT YOU DO

1. Cover the bulletin board with the white paper.

2. Have the children work together to create a beautiful mountain scene including sun, trees, and water.

3. Cut letters for the title "GOD IS" from purple paper.

4. Ask the students to think of words that describe God. Let them print the words on strips of paper and mount the word strips on the board.

WHAT YOU TALK ABOUT

Ask the students what words they would use to describe themselves. Ask, "What words can we use that show how God is different and greater than any person?"

WHAT YOU NEED

Gold or silver gift-wrap
Construction paper (dark and light blue)
Scissors
Dark colored markers

WHAT YOU DO

1. Cover the board with gold or silver gift-wrap

2. Cut letters for the first part of the caption from dark blue paper and mount them on the board as shown.

3. Cut fat letters for the words PROMISE KEEPER from light blue paper.

4. Talk about some of God's promises in the Bible.

5. Hand out the light blue letters and markers. Let the children print one of God's promises on each of the letters. (Ask each student to tell what he is going to write to avoid duplication.)

6. Mount the letters on the board as shown.

WHAT YOU TALK ABOUT

Talk about God's promises to people in the Bible and to us today. Discuss how He kept each promise. Point out that we are still waiting for Him to keep some of His promises, such as Jesus' promise to come again. Remind students that God has never broken a promise.

Joseph knew
What to do,
And God wants you
To do it too.

"Love the Lord your God with all your heart and with all your soul and with all your strength." Deuteronomy 6:5

WHAT YOU NEED

Construction paper (white and tan)
Scissors
Figure of Joseph from page 153
Dark colored marker

WHAT YOU DO

1. Use a dark colored marker to print the rhyme on a white piece of paper. Mount it on the left side of the board.

2. Draw two or three pyramids on tan paper and cut them out. Place them on the board as shown.

3. Mount the figure of Joseph on the right side of the board.

4. Print the Bible verse, Deuteronomy 6:5, on a strip of white or tan paper and attach it to the bottom of the board.

WHAT YOU TALK ABOUT

Have a volunteer read the rhyme aloud. Discuss how Joseph showed that he loved God with all his heart, soul, and strength. Have students tell ways their thoughts and actions would be different if they obeyed the verse as Joseph did.

WHAT YOU NEED

White paper
Colored construction paper (including black)
Colored markers (including black)
Scissors

WHAT YOU DO

1. Cut out letters for the title "God Cared for Moses" and mount them on the center of the board.

2. Cut large black arrows from construction paper.

3. Hand out white paper and colored markers. Have students draw scenes from Moses' life as shown on the board. Assign a scene to each student or pair of students.

4. Help the students mount their drawings in order around the board as shown. Then let them mount the black arrows between the drawings.
OPTION: Have students use cut paper or torn paper to create the scenes from Moses' life.

WHAT YOU TALK ABOUT

Ask students to tell about the scenes they drew and explain how God cared for Moses. Ask them to share ways God has cared for them.

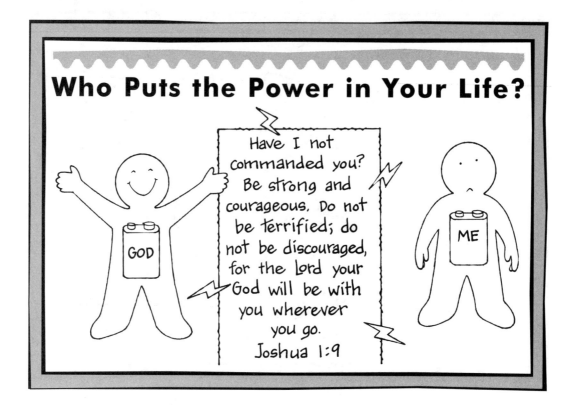

WHAT YOU NEED

Construction paper (red and orange)

Scissors

Black marker

2 9-volt or other flat batteries

Figures of children from page 146,
enlarged and copied

Glue or tape

WHAT YOU DO

1 Cut letters for the caption from red construction paper and mount them on the bulletin board as shown.

2 Print Joshua 1:9 on orange paper and mount it at the center of the board.

3 Attach the figures of the children on the board as shown.

4 Glue or tape the appropriate label to each battery and attach the battery to the child on the board.

WHAT YOU TALK ABOUT

Ask students if they ever feel weak or afraid. Read Joshua 1:9 from the board. Point out that God wants to help us as He helped Joshua. Ask students how they can have God's power in their lives.

The Lord Is My Shepherd I Will Trust Him

WHAT YOU NEED

Construction paper (green, white, and black)

Scissors

Figure of Jesus the Good Shepherd from page 145

Pencils and markers

Craft materials (cotton, tissue paper, pasta)

WHAT YOU DO

1. Cut the letters for the caption from green paper and mount them across the top of the board.

2. Hand out pencils, markers, scissors, white and black paper, and craft materials. Let students create sheep, each using their own ideas.

3. Mount the figure of the Good Shepherd on the board.

4. Have the students put their names on their sheep and mount them on the board around the Good Shepherd.

WHAT YOU TALK ABOUT

Read Psalm 23 together; then discuss how Jesus is the Good Shepherd and we are His sheep. Point out that just as all the sheep on the board are different and unique, so are we. Our Good Shepherd knows each of us better than anyone else does. We can trust Him because He knows what we need and how to care for us.

When Your Life Breaks Apart, Let God Rebuild It!

His Word

Job list
Pray
Read the Bible
Do right

Mercy

Grace

Peace

Forgiveness

Love

WHAT YOU NEED

- Construction paper (brown and tan)
- Scissors
- Black marker
- Building tools (real ones or pictures cut from a catalog)
- Real nails

WHAT YOU DO

1. Cut letters for the caption from brown paper and mount them at the top and bottom of the board.

2. Attach tools and nails to the board. For heavy items, use straightened out wire coat hangers. Wrap the wire around the object, then bend the other end of the wire and hang it over the top of the board so that the object hangs in the proper place on the board.

3. Write "Job List" on a piece of tan paper and attach it to the board. Ask students what they think their jobs are in helping to build up their lives. Offer suggestions as needed. Print their answers on the list.

4. Ask students what God gives us that helps us when we have problems in our lives. Give them label strips and have them print a separate idea on each strip. Help them attach each label beneath a tool on the board.

WHAT YOU TALK ABOUT

Give students examples of troubles they might face. Use examples of troubles they might bring on themselves, such as lying, and examples of circumstances beyond their control, such as the death of a grandparent. Ask them to tell what jobs they could do to help in those times. Then help them decide what tools God could provide to help.

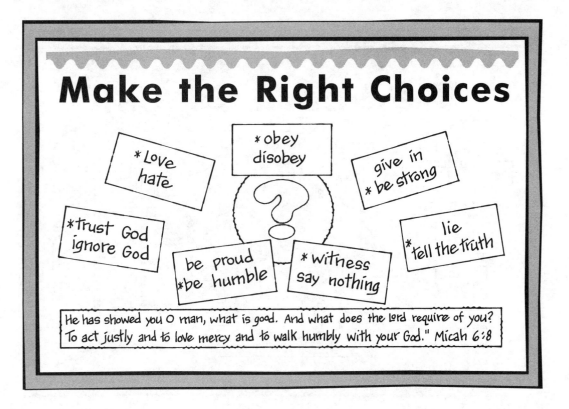

Make the Right Choices

*Love hate

*obey disobey

give in *be strong

*trust God ignore God

be proud *be humble

*witness say nothing

lie *tell the truth

He has showed you O man, what is good. And what does the Lord require of you? To act justly and to love mercy and to walk humbly with your God." Micah 6:8

WHAT YOU NEED

Construction paper (various colors
  including black and white)
Scissors
Black and red markers

WHAT YOU DO

1. Cut letters for the caption from black construction paper and mount them on the board.

2. Print Micah 6:8 on a strip of colored paper and mount it across the bottom of the board.

3. Hand out white paper and black markers. Have students write down choices between right and wrong that they have to make every day. Have them use the format shown on the board.

4. Help the students mount each choice on colored construction paper, then on the board.

5. Go over the choices on the board. Let students say what the correct choices should be. Draw a large red * next to each correct choice.

WHAT YOU TALK ABOUT

Ask students what things they can do to help them make right choices. Ask students what happens when they depend on their own understanding or preferences to make hard choices. God wants to help us, through His Holy Spirit, make good choices and not yield to the temptation to do wrong.

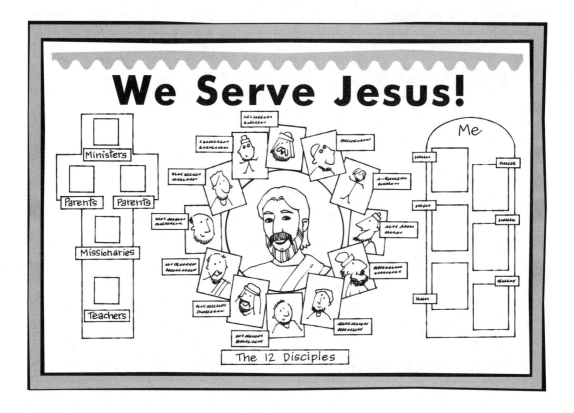

We Serve Jesus!

Ministers
Parents Parents
Missionaries
Teachers

Me

The 12 Disciples

WHAT YOU NEED

Blue paper
Yellow and white construction paper
Colored markers (including black)
Scissors
Figure of Jesus from page 145
Photos of students, church staff, and
    others as shown on the board

WHAT YOU DO

1. Cover the bulletin board with blue paper.

2. Cut letters for the caption from yellow paper and mount them on the board as shown.

3. Mount the figure of Jesus at the center of the board.

4. Hand out white paper and markers. Have students draw the faces of the twelve disciples. (Assign each student a disciple to avoid duplication.) Mount the disciples around the figure of Jesus on the board.

5. Mount photos or self-portraits of the students on a sheet of yellow paper and mount it on the board as shown. Place the label "ME" above the photos.

6. Mount photos of your church staff, some of the students' parents, missionaries, and teachers from your church on the board with labels under them.

WHAT YOU TALK ABOUT

Talk about Jesus' disciples, emphasizing that they were ordinary people who did extraordinary things as God used them. He wants to use us too. Discuss some of the ways God has used your ministers, students' parents, missionaries, and so on. Ask students to share what they would like to do for Jesus.

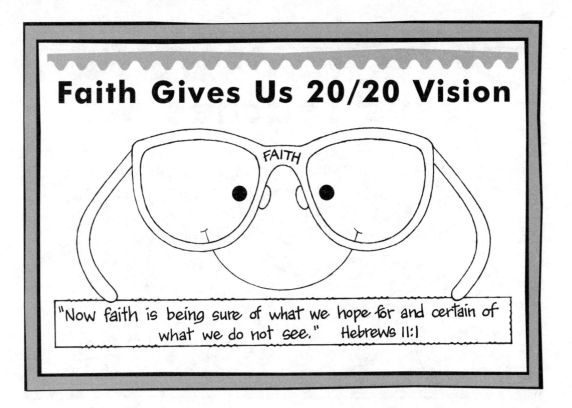

Faith Gives Us 20/20 Vision

FAITH

"Now faith is being sure of what we hope for and certain of what we do not see."   Hebrews 11:1

WHAT YOU NEED
Construction paper (purple, pink, and white)
Scissors
Black marker

WHAT YOU DO

1. Cut letters for the caption from purple paper and mount them on the board as shown.

2. Print Hebrews 11:1 on a strip of white paper and mount it at the bottom of the board.

3. Cut a large pair of eyeglasses from pink paper, enlarging the pattern from the board. Print the word FAITH on them. Mount the glasses on the board.

WHAT YOU TALK ABOUT
Ask students to read Hebrews 11:1 with you. Ask, "What do you hope for? What do you hope for from God?" Ask, "What are some things we believe about God that we cannot see?"

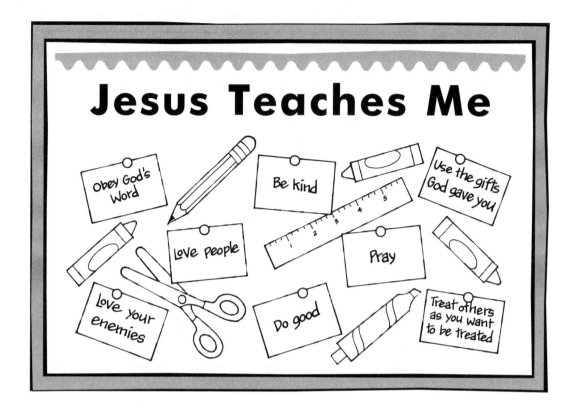

WHAT YOU NEED

- White ruled paper
- Scissors
- Colored index cards
- Colored markers
- School supplies (ruler, markers, pencils, scissors, eraser, and so on)

WHAT YOU DO

1. Cut letters for the caption from white ruled paper and mount them on the board as shown. You may wish to cover the board with dark paper to make the letters stand out.

2. Hand out index cards and markers. Have students print one thing on each card that they've learned from Jesus. Scatter the cards over the board.

3. Attach the school supplies to the board.

WHAT YOU TALK ABOUT

Talk about what you learn from Jesus each week. Have students make new cards to add to the board as they learn new things from Jesus.

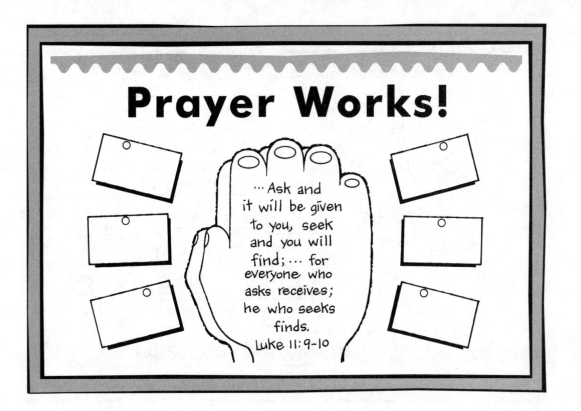

Prayer Works!

...Ask and it will be given to you, seek and you will find; ... for everyone who asks receives; he who seeks finds.
Luke 11: 9-10

WHAT YOU NEED
- Construction paper (red, white)
- Scissors
- 4" x 6" pieces of paper or cards with praying hands in the corner (use praying hands stickers)
- Markers (red and black)

WHAT YOU DO

1. Cut letters for the caption from red paper and mount them on the board.

2. Copy the Bible verses on white paper using a red marker. Mount the paper at the center of the board.

3. Hand out markers and 4" x 6" paper or cards. Have students write or draw pictures of prayers God has answered for them and mount them on the board.
OPTION: Keep blank prayer cards. Print requests on the cards and pray for the requests each week. As prayers are answered, attach the cards to the board.

WHAT YOU TALK ABOUT
Talk about prayers God has answered for you. Then ask students to share. Say a prayer, encouraging children to thank God for the answered prayers on their cards.

If God could help Peter...
- preach a sermon
- heal a lame man
- witness to his enemies
- raise the dead
- learn an important lesson
- escape from prison

I know God can help me!

WHAT YOU NEED

Yellow paper
Scissors
Black marker

WHAT YOU DO

1. Print the captions on long strips of yellow paper and mount them across the top and bottom of the board.

2. Enlarge and cut out the figure of Peter from the board above. Mount the figure of Peter on the left of the board.

3. Print on six yellow strips of paper the things God helped Peter do as shown on the board.

4. Show students the strips of paper and have them tell about each incident. Then ask them to draw simple sketches to on the right side of the strips to illustrate each item. (Use samples on board.)

WHAT YOU TALK ABOUT

Remind students that Peter was an ordinary person, but because he gave his life to God, he was able to do wonderful things. If God could help Peter, can't He also help us do whatever He wants us to? Ask students to name some of the things they think God wants them to do with His help.

WHAT YOU NEED
Construction paper (yellow, black, brown)
Scissors
Black marker
Bee pattern from page 150

WHAT YOU DO

1 Cut letters for the caption from black paper and mount them on the board.

2 Enlarge and copy the beehive from the board on brown paper, cut it out, and mount it at the center of the board.

3 Enlarge and copy several bees on yellow paper and cut them out.

4 Print on each bee one of the attitudes God wants us to have (see the board). Mount them on the board.

5 Hand out bees to your students. Let them write on the bees other things God wants us to be and add them to the board.

WHAT YOU TALK ABOUT
Read Galatians 5:22, 23. Ask students to name some attitudes God wants us to have from those verses. Talk about how they could demonstrate each of those attitudes.

WHAT YOU NEED

Construction paper (dark blue, light green, and white)

Scissors

Colored markers (including dark blue)

WHAT YOU DO

1. Cut letters for the caption from dark blue paper and mount them at the top of the board.

2. Print Psalm 119:90a on a piece of light green paper and attach it to the center of the board.

3. Hand out white paper and colored markers. Have students draw pictures of Old Testament people who proved God's faithfulness: Abraham, Isaac, Jacob and Esau, Deborah, Gideon, King Saul, Samuel, Elijah, and so on.

4. Mount the pictures all around the board as shown to make a photo gallery.

5. Give students construction paper, markers, and glue, and ask them to cut and design creative frames for the gallery photos. Help them attach the frames around each picture.

WHAT YOU TALK ABOUT

Ask students to share briefly the stories of their favorite Old Testament people. Talk about how God showed His faithfulness to each one. Ask them to name ways God shows His faithfulness to us today. For example, He kept His promise to send Jesus His Son. He sends His Holy Spirit to help us. He forgives every wrong we do. He still sends His rainbow to remind us there will be no more great floods.

God's Greatest Gift

"For God so loved the world that he gave his one and only Son, that whoever believes in him shall not perish but have eternal life. For God did not send his Son into the world to condemn the world, but to save the world through him."
John 3:16-17

WHAT YOU NEED
- Construction paper (white and green)
- Scissors
- Flat box
- Birthday gift-wrap and ribbon
- Red marker
- Glue
- Pictures of manger scene and wise men scene (from Christmas cards or Sunday school lessons)
- Thank-you postcards or colored index cards
- Pens or pencils

WHAT YOU DO
1. Cut letters for the caption from green paper and mount them on the board as shown.

2. Gift-wrap a flat box. Wrap the top of the box separately so it can be taken off. Mount the box on the board with the top facing out.

3. Using a red marker, print John 3:16, 17 on a piece of white paper the same size as the box. Take off the top of the box and glue or tape the verses inside. Then put the top of the box back on.

4. Print a gift tag on a small piece of paper saying "TO: You, FROM: God." Attach the tag to the gift box.

5. Color and add the manger scene and wise men to the board as shown.

6. Hand out the postcards or index cards and pens or pencils. Have student create thank-You notes to God for the gift of His Son. Then ask them to mount the notes on the board.

WHAT YOU TALK ABOUT
Ask students to share the best Christmas gifts they ever received. Then point out that the very best Christmas gift ever given was the gift of God's Son to the world. No other gift has ever compared to it. Have a thank-you time, asking students to read their thank-you notes to God.

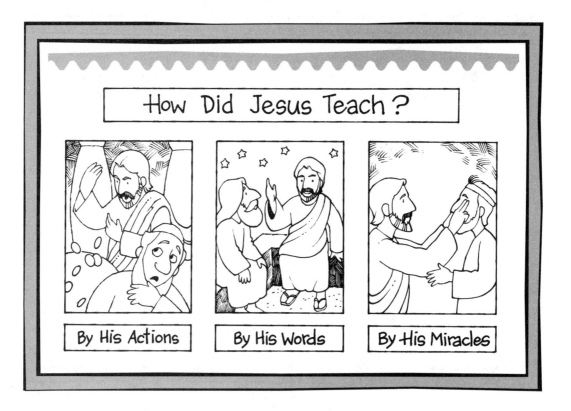

How Did Jesus Teach?

By His Actions   By His Words   By His Miracles

WHAT YOU NEED
White paper
Colored markers (including black)

WHAT YOU DO

1 Print the caption on a strip of white paper and mount it across the top of the board.

2 Divide students into groups of two or three. Assign each group one of the pictures above to draw. (Everyone in a group should contribute to the group picture—planning, drawing, or coloring.) When the pictures are done, help students mount them on the board.

3 Print labels for the pictures on white paper and mount them under the pictures as shown.

WHAT YOU TALK ABOUT
Discuss the three Bible stories: Jesus clearing the temple, Jesus with Nicodemus, and Jesus healing people. Talk about how Jesus was teaching people when He did these things. Ask students to think of some other ways Jesus taught people about God.

Follow me.

Blessed are you.

Sit down and eat.

Don't be afraid.

WHAT YOU NEED

- White paper
- Pencils
- Colored markers
- Figure of Jesus from page 144
- Plasti-tak or Velcro
- Scissors
- Glue
- Construction paper

WHAT YOU DO

1 Cut a sheet of white paper large enough to cover the bulletin board and divide it into four sections.

2 Divide students into four drawing teams. Give each team pencils, colored markers, scissors, glue, and construction paper. Assign each team a Scripture and ask them to create a scene from that Scripture on the large paper. Scriptures for each team follow. Team one: John 1:43-50; Luke 6:12-16; Team two: Matthew 5:1-12; Team three: Matthew 8:23-27; Team four: John 6:1-14. The students may draw their scenes and/or cut out figures to glue to the paper for the scene.

3 When the scenes are done, attach the paper to the bulletin board. Attach the figure of Jesus to the center of the board, using Plasti-tak or Velcro.

4 Ask the teams to take turn moving the figure of Jesus to their scene and explaining what Jesus taught.
OPTION: If you are using the board throughout a unit of stories, move the figure of Jesus each week to the scene you are studying.

WHAT YOU TALK ABOUT

Ask the students to name ways they can do what Jesus taught in each of the four Scriptures.

[glove]-G the Lord U+R God with [baseball]-B U+R [heart] [hand]-H [baseball]-B U+R [foot]-+L [hand]-H with [baseball]-B U+R [lightbulb face]. This is the 1ST [hand]-H GREATEST [tablets] [hand]-H the 2nd is like it: [glove]-G U+R neighbor as U+R+self. Matthew 22:37-39

WHAT YOU NEED
Large piece of paper or poster board
Light-colored construction paper
Scissors
Colored markers (including black)

WHAT YOU DO

1 Print out Matthew 22:37-39 on a large piece of paper or poster board. Ask students to come up with pictures for some of the words. Use the board as an example. Draw the students' ideas on the paper.

2 Assign each student or group of students a word or picture to carefully letter or draw on a strip of paper.

3 Help students mount the strips of paper in order on the bulletin board.

WHAT YOU TALK ABOUT
Have a volunteer read the verses on the bulletin board aloud. Discuss what it means to love the Lord with all your heart, soul, and mind. Then talk about practical ways to love your neighbors.

WHAT YOU NEED

Newspapers
Paper (black and white)
Scissors
Black markers and pens

WHAT YOU DO

1 Cover the board with newspaper.

2 Cut letters for the caption from black paper and mount them on the board.

3 Divide students into small groups and give them white paper and black markers and pens. Assign each group a story to report in a newspaper that they create. The stories are Jesus' death, burial, resurrection, and ascension. Remind students to include exciting headlines and illustrations if possible.

4 Mount the newspaper stories on the board.

WHAT YOU TALK ABOUT

Talk about how the events of Jesus' last days on earth would be covered in newspapers if they happened today. Would the reports be slanted? In what way? Who would be interviewed? Which stories would make the front page? To whom could they report the news about Jesus?

The Seeds of the Church

WHAT YOU NEED

Construction paper (green, brown, white, and yellow)
Scissors
Black marker
Glue
Seed packets and sunflower seeds

WHAT YOU DO

1. Cut letters for the caption from green paper and mount them at the top of the board.

2. Cut a large sunflower from yellow, green, and brown paper. Print on it "GOD'S CHURCH" and attach it to the center of the board.

3. Cut a large sun from yellow paper and mount it on the board. Add some grass made from green paper at the bottom of the board.

4. Print the names of Paul, Philip, and Stephen on small pieces of white paper and glue them on the seed packets. Mount the seed packets on the board.

5. Glue real sunflower seeds on the board near the seed packets and on the grass.

WHAT YOU TALK ABOUT

Ask the students to share how Paul, Philip, and Stephen helped the church grow. Ask them to think of ways they can help the church grow.

WHAT YOU NEED

Large map of the world (or of the Near East)

Black construction paper

Scissors

Figure of Paul from page 149, enlarged and copied

Fine-tip colored markers or pens

Ruled paper

WHAT YOU DO

1. Cover the board with the map.

2. Cut words for the caption from black paper and mount them across the top of the board.

3. Mount the figure of Paul at the center of the board.

4. Hand out ruled paper and fine-tip colored markers or pens. Have students write letters from Paul about his experiences in Iconium, Lystra, Philippi, Troas, Jerusalem, and Caesarea.

5. Mount the letters on the board.
OPTION: If you are studying a different place Paul traveled each week, have students write letters each week as you study his experiences.

WHAT YOU TALK ABOUT

Talk about some of the places Paul traveled. Discuss what happened to him in each place. Ask students why they think Paul continued traveling to preach the Gospel even when he was mistreated, put into prison, and chased out of town. Ask them to share some things that have happened to them, both good and bad, when they have told others about Jesus.

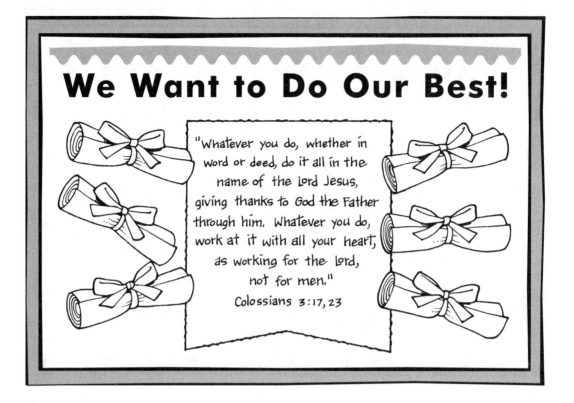

We Want to Do Our Best!

"Whatever you do, whether in word or deed, do it all in the name of the Lord Jesus, giving thanks to God the Father through him. Whatever you do, work at it with all your heart, as working for the Lord, not for men."
Colossians 3:17, 23

WHAT YOU NEED
Construction paper (dark blue and gold)
Scissors
Dark blue marker
White paper
Thin ribbon

WHAT YOU DO

1. Cut letters for the caption from dark blue paper and mount them across the top of the board.

2. Print Colossians 3:17, 23 on gold paper and mount it on the board as shown.

3. On a piece of white paper, print or type the following promise. "Whatever I do, whether in word or deed, I will do it all in the name of the Lord Jesus, giving thanks to God the Father through him. Whatever I do, I will work at it with all my heart, as working for the Lord, nor for men." Make enough copies of the paper for each student to have one.

4. Give students the papers. Ask them to write or draw how they will do their best and sign their name on the papers.

5. Have students roll up their paper and tie them with a ribbon. Then attach the contracts to the board.

WHAT YOU TALK ABOUT
Share a way that you have done your best for God. Each week, ask students to share times they have done their best for God.

WHAT YOU NEED

- Construction paper (gold and white)
- Scissors
- Black marker
- Figure of Jesus from page 144, enlarged and copied
- Craft materials (cotton, glitter, glue, white paper doilies, felt, white cardboard)

WHAT YOU DO

1. Cut letters for the caption from gold paper and mount them at the top of the board.

2. Mount the figure of Jesus at the center of the board. Under the figure mount a piece of gold paper on which you have printed "I am coming soon!"

3. Hand out paper and craft materials to students. Let each student create an angel of his own design. Attach the completed angels to the board.

4. Attach cotton clouds around the board to give the idea of heaven.

WHAT YOU TALK ABOUT

Ask students to share their thoughts and feelings about Jesus' return. Is it an event to look forward to? Be frightened about? Wonder about? Ask them to describe what they think heaven will be like. (Read Revelation 22 for an accurate description of heaven.) Ask them what they think they'll do in heaven. Explain that the Bible says we will praise the Lord with the angels.

As children mature, teachers and parents need to use more creative ideas and methods for teaching Bible stories, truths, and concepts to them. Since they've often studied the same Bible story or passage many times before, preteens may feel that they already know them and don't need to go over them again. Bulletin boards can help put a new spin on familiar stories and truths (see page 97). They can also give students opportunity to personalize a truth and see it in practical, relevant terms (see page 86).

The bulletin boards on the following 26 pages emphasize the relevancy of God's Word and provide practical ways for preteens to walk with the Lord and serve Him every day at church, home, and school. Some students will be eager to help you put together the bulletin boards; others will seem uninterested. Try to involve them in interesting ways—not just cutting out letters for a caption, but deciding how the items on a board should be arranged or what could be added to the board to make it even more effective. Use each board as a discussion starter as well as an attention getter. Encourage a classroom atmosphere of acceptance so students feel free to ask questions and share opinions without fear of being put down by you or fellow students.

Many of these bulletin boards contain challenges for your preteens. The captions are usually short and may be remembered by students long after the board has been taken down. Pray that the Lord would use these short messages to remind preteens of the challenge of living for Him in their everyday lives.

WHAT YOU NEED

Light blue and dark blue paper
Photos or drawings of students
Post-it notes
Markers

WHAT YOU DO

1 Cover the bulletin board with light blue paper.

2 Cut letters for the caption from dark blue paper. Mount them across the top of the board.

3 Mount photos of everyone in the class on the board. Or ask students to draw themselves and mount the pictures on the board.

4 Hand out Post-it notes and markers. Ask your students to think about special gifts or personality characteristics for each person in the class. They should write the one or two word descriptions on Post-it notes and stick them next to each person's picture. Emphasize that they should focus on positive, encouraging descriptions.

WHAT YOU TALK ABOUT

Talk about ways God uses your special gifts for Him. Share other examples of adults the children know. Ask them to name ways they can use their gifts to serve God.

Be a Homerun Hitter in Your Christian Life

Make choices that honor God

Resist temptation

Confess your sins

Ask God for forgiveness

Do the right thing

WHAT YOU NEED
Construction paper (brown and white)
Scissors
Black marker

WHAT YOU DO

1 Cut letters for the caption from brown paper and mount them on the board as shown.

2 Cut a baseball bat from brown paper, enlarging the pattern on the board.

3 Cut five large baseballs from white paper Print on each baseball one of the ways to hit a home run in the Christian life.

4 Mount the bat and balls on the board.
OPTION: Provide baseballs and a black marker. Ask students to name specific ways they can please God and be homerun hitters. Print their answers on the balls. Keep the balls in a bucket or other container by the bulletin board. Each week, ask students to share ways they have done the things written on the board and on the balls. At the end of the unit, give each student a ball to take home.

WHAT YOU TALK ABOUT
Ask students to think about the Christian life in terms of a baseball game. Whose team are we playing on? (God's) What happens when we do wrong? (We strike out.) What happens when we obey God and live to please Him? (We hit home runs.) Discuss the things God expects us to do (on the baseballs). What happens when a player is always striking out? (The whole team suffers.) Let students add their own ideas about hitting home runs for the Lord.

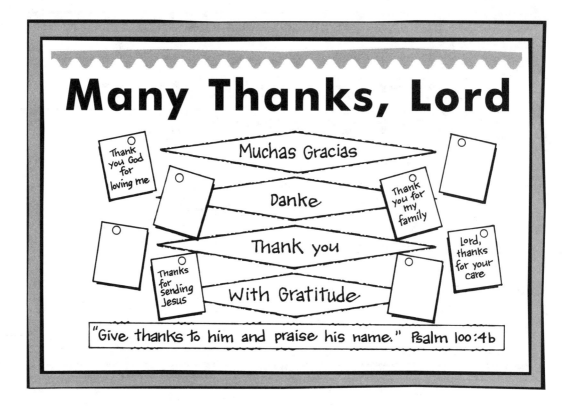

WHAT YOU NEED

Construction paper (a variety of colors)
Scissors
Dark colored markers

WHAT YOU DO

1. Cut letters for the caption from bright colored construction paper and mount them on the board.

2. Cut shapes as shown on the bulletin board and print a different way to say thank you on each shape. Mount the words on the board.

3. Cut 3" x 5" pieces of colored paper and hand them out to students with dark colored markers. Have them write thank-You notes to God.

4. Scatter the thank-You notes all over the board.

5. Print Psalm 100:4b on a strip of paper and mount it at the bottom of the board.

WHAT YOU TALK ABOUT

Tell your students something for which you are thankful to God. Ask them to share their reasons for thanking Him. Ask them to think of other ways we can thank God besides writing Him thank-You notes.

Do You Know His Name?

Immanuel · Son of God · Savior · Prince of Peace · Wonderful Counselor · Everlasting Father

WHAT YOU NEED

White paper

Construction paper (red and green)

Colored markers (including black)

Figures of shepherds, sheep, and baby Jesus from page 150, enlarged and copied

WHAT YOU DO

1. Color the figures you have copied. Draw a stable and background as shown and mount the figures on the board to make a manger scene.

2. Cut letters for the caption from red paper and mount them at the top of the board.

3. Ask students to call out different names for Jesus. Have them look up Isaiah 9:6 for a list of some names. Ask students to print the names in large letters on strips of red and green paper and mount them on the board.

WHAT YOU TALK ABOUT

Discuss the names for Jesus on the board. Ask students to think of others. Talk about the meaning of each name. Ask students to tell their favorite names for Jesus and explain why.

WHAT YOU NEED

Construction paper (green, brown,
    yellow, red, gray or white)
Scissors
Black marker
Red or pink tissue paper
Clear tape
Water can and seed bag patterns from
    page 145

WHAT YOU TALK ABOUT

Ask students what is needed for a climbing rose
or vine to grow and be healthy. Compare
Christians to a vine. What do Christians need to
grow into the kind of people God wants us to
be? Refer to the words on the bulletin board.

WHAT YOU DO

1. Cut letters for the caption from green construction paper and mount them on the bulletin board as shown.

2. Cut a large sun from yellow paper. Print on it "Let Your Light Shine." Mount the sun on the board.

3. Using the patterns, cut a water can and a seed bag from gray or white paper. Print on the can "Pour on the Prayer." Print on the bag "Feed on God's Word." Mount the can and bag on the board as shown.

4. Cut a trellis from brown paper. Print on it "Be Supported by Other Believers." Mount it on the right side of the board.

5. Cut vines from green paper and attach them to the trellis. Hand out tissue paper and tape. Have the students make paper flowers and attach them to the vines.
OPTION: Provide seed packets, paper cups or small plastic pots, and potting soil. Ask students name specific things they need to do to grow for Jesus. Ask them to write ways they will grow on their packets. Help the students fill their cups or pots with soil and plant a few seeds from their packet in the soil. When the seeds are planted, have them tape the packet to the front of their cups or pots to remind them of the ways they will grow.

The World Will Know Us by Our LOVE

"My command is this: Love each other as I have loved you."   John 15:12

WHAT YOU NEED

Construction paper (red, white, light colors)
Scissors
Fine tip black markers
Items to decorate hearts (paper doilies, ribbon, bits of lace and rickrack, scraps of material, stickers)
Glue

WHAT YOU DO

1. Cut the letters for the caption from red paper and mount them across the top of the board.

2. Print John 15:12 on a strip of white paper and mount it at the bottom of the board.

3. Hand out construction paper, scissors, markers, items for decorating hearts, and glue. Have the students cut hearts out of various colors of construction paper and decorate them using the items you provided.

4. On each heart, have a student print a Bible verse about love. Mount the hearts on the board. Suggested verses follow: Ephesians 4:29; Ephesians 4:32; Ephesians 5:2; Matthew 25:35, 36; James 2:18; 1 Corinthians 13:4, 5, 6, 7, 13.
OPTION: Have students make their own hearts to take home with them. On the hearts, ask them to write the ways they will show love this week.

WHAT YOU TALK ABOUT

Discuss the ways to show love mentioned in the Scriptures. (Tell others about Jesus; help those in need; do what you believe; demonstrate the characteristics of love.) Ask students to share specific ways they can show love at home, at school, with their friends.

When the going gets tough, God is more than enough! Have faith in Him.

WHAT YOU NEED

Construction paper (light purple, gray, and white)
Colored markers
Scissors
Figure of mountain climber from page 153, enlarged and copied
Small piece of twine

WHAT YOU DO

1 Print the caption on a piece of light purple paper and attach it to the left side of the board.

2 Cut a mountain shape from gray paper and attach it to the right side of the board.

3 Color the mountain climber and mount him on the board as shown.

4 Attach a small piece of twine to the board for the rope the mountain climber is hanging on to.

WHAT YOU TALK ABOUT

Have a volunteer read the rhyme on the board. Discuss some rough things in life that may make us want to give up (discouragement, sickness, failure, and so on). Briefly review some Bible people who demonstrated faith in God during difficult times. (See Hebrews 11.) Share a time when it was tough for you to have faith. Ask students to share some difficult times they have had.

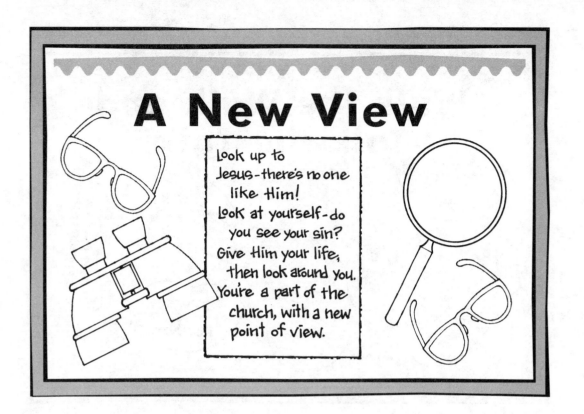

A New View

Look up to Jesus—there's no one like Him!
Look at yourself—do you see your sin?
Give Him your life, then look around you.
You're a part of the church, with a new point of view.

WHAT YOU NEED

- Blue paper
- Construction paper (gold and white)
- Scissors
- Black marker
- Real viewing tools (glasses, magnifying glass, binoculars, and so on)

WHAT YOU DO

1. Cover the board with blue paper.

2. Cut letters for the caption from gold paper and mount them at the top of the board.

3. Print the poem on white paper and mount it at the center of the board.

4. Attach the viewing tools around the poem. If you need help mounting the tools, use straightened out wire coat hangers. Wind the wire around the tool, then hook the other end of the wire across the top of the board, so that the tool hangs in the right place on the board.

WHAT YOU TALK ABOUT

Ask students what we should be viewing with our tools if we want to have a new view. Read Hebrews 12:2 together. Ask students what things they can do to keep their eyes on Jesus.

WHAT YOU NEED

Construction paper (brown, pink, and red)

Scissors

Pencils

Black markers

WHAT YOU DO

1. Cut letters for the caption from red construction paper and mount them on the board.

2. Hand out brown, pink, and red paper, pencils, and black markers. Have students take their shoes off and trace their feet (one per student) on brown or pink paper. They should print one of the admonitions from Romans 12:9, 10, 13 on each foot, cut it out, and mount it on the board.

3. Have them cut lips out of red and pink paper, write admonitions on them from Scripture about how to speak, and mount them on the board. (See the ideas on the board.)

WHAT YOU TALK ABOUT

Read Romans 12:9, 10, 13 together. Ask students to share ways they have done some of the things listed in the verses. Discuss ways the students could put these ideas into action this month.

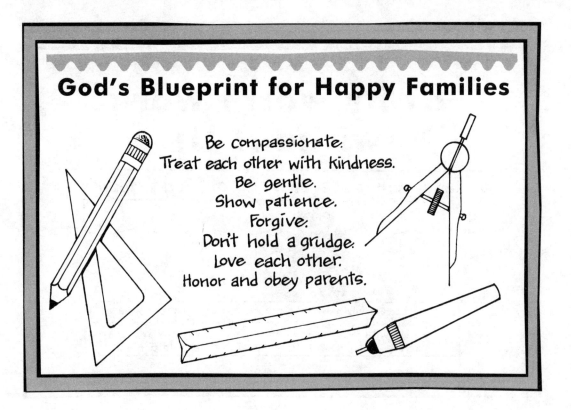

God's Blueprint for Happy Families

Be compassionate.
Treat each other with kindness.
Be gentle.
Show patience.
Forgive.
Don't hold a grudge.
Love each other.
Honor and obey parents.

WHAT YOU NEED
Blue paper
Black marker
Architect tools (T-square, pencil, triangle, compass, and so on)

WHAT YOU DO

1 Cover the board with blue paper.

2 Print the caption at the top of the board on the blue paper.

3 At the center of the blue paper print the list of actions and attitudes families should have toward one another, taken from Colossians 3:12-14.

4 Attach architect tools around the list as shown. If you need help attaching the tools, use straightened out wire coat hangers. Wrap the wire around the tool, then hook the other end over the top of the board, so that the tool hangs in the right place on the board.

WHAT YOU TALK ABOUT
Discuss the actions on the board. Ask students to share ways they would treat their parents if they obeyed the actions on the board. How would they treat their older sisters and brothers? Younger sisters and brothers?

Unity won't work without U!

Take your place as part of God's team.

"May the God who gives endurance and encouragement give you a spirit of unity among yourselves as you follow Christ Jesus, so that with one heart and mouth you may glorify the God and Father of our lord Jesus Christ." Romans 15:5-6

WHAT YOU NEED
Black construction paper
White paper
Scissors
Red and dark markers
Tape

WHAT YOU DO

1. Cut letters for the caption from black paper and mount them on the board as shown.

2. Print the sub caption on white paper using a red marker and mount it under the caption.

3. Print Romans 15:5, 6 on a strip of white paper and mount it at the bottom of the board.

4. Accordion fold a strip of white paper. Draw the outline of a person on it and cut it out, being sure not to cut across either fold. Unfold the paper to get a strip of connected people. Make enough to reach from one side of the board to the other. Make two extra strips of figures to use as you discuss the board with the students.

5. Tape the figures together and color the center figure a dark color. Mount them across the board as shown.

WHAT YOU TALK ABOUT
Read the Bible verses together. Discuss what unity means. Ask students what kinds of things destroy unity, such as gossip, unkind actions, anger, judging others, and so on. As they name problems, print their ideas on one strip of figures and cut them apart, so that they fall to the floor. Then ask students to name actions that promote unity. Print their ideas on the second set of figures. Keep the figures by the bulletin board as a reminder of the ways we can be part of God's team.

God Uses Ordinary People to Do Extraordinary Things

WHAT YOU NEED

Construction paper (orange and white)
Scissors
Figures of Peter and John, and Paul from page 153
Colored markers

WHAT YOU DO

1. Cut letters for the caption from orange paper and mount them across the top of the board.

2. Mount the pictures of Peter and John, and Paul on the board as shown.

3. Hand out white paper and markers. Have students draw pictures of ordinary people they know or have heard of who have been used of God. (Examples: the people who led them to Christ, a Sunday school teacher, a missionary, and so on.) At the bottom of each picture should be a brief explanation of how God used that person. Mount the pictures on the board.

WHAT YOU TALK ABOUT

Ask students to tell about people they know who have been used by God in other people's lives. You may want to get the discussion started by telling about someone you have known and how God used that person.

Friendship with Jesus makes every friendship better!

"Greater love has no one than this, that he lay down his life for his friends." John 15:13

WHAT YOU NEED

Construction paper (black and yellow)
Scissors
Black fine tip markers or pens
Figure of Jesus from page 144

WHAT YOU DO

1. Cut letters for the caption from black paper and mount them at the top of the board.

2. Mount the figure of Jesus at the center of the board.

3. Print John 15:13 on a strip of yellow paper and mount it under the figure of Jesus.

4. Hand out circles of yellow paper and markers or pens. Have students write on the circles how God has blessed them with good friends and what those friends have done for them. Mount the circles on the board.

WHAT YOU TALK ABOUT

Let students talk about their friends, including specific examples of how God has blessed them in their friendships. Ask students how Jesus is their best friend. Is a friendship between Christians different than a friendship between a Christian and an unbeliever? Why?

YOU HAVE TWO CHOICES:

Believe that God created you in His image   OR   Make a monkey out of yourself

WHAT YOU NEED

Construction paper (red and white)
Scissors
Black marker
Picture of a preteen and picture of a monkey from page 154 (or cut from magazines)

WHAT YOU DO

1 Cut letters for the caption from red paper and mount them on the board.

2 Print the two choices on white paper and mount it on the board as shown.

3 Enlarge and copy the figures from page 154. Color them and mount the picture of the preteen on the left side of the board and the monkey on the right.

WHAT YOU TALK ABOUT

Ask students to share what they learn at school from secular textbooks about the origins of people. Discuss the biblical account of creation. You may wish to print contrasting ideas on slips of paper and mount them on the board. For example, evolution says that each new type of animals evolved slowly over millions of years. Creationists believe that God created each new type of animal completely formed. As you discover scientific proofs for the ideas, add them to the list.

FACE THE CHALLENGE: STAND UP FOR THE LORD!

Speak boldly
Take a stand for right
Always put God first
Never compromise
Depend on God for strength and courage

WHAT YOU NEED
Construction paper (blue and light green)
Scissors
Dark blue marker

WHAT YOU DO
1. Cut letters for the caption from blue paper and mount them at the top and bottom of the board.

2. Print the acrostic on light green paper and mount it at the center of the board. (Be sure to make the first letter of each line bigger and bolder than the others.)

WHAT YOU TALK ABOUT
Discuss the ways of standing up for the Lord listed on the board. Ask students to share other ways they have stood up for the Lord. Talk about what makes it hard to stand up for the Lord (fear of being different, shyness, lack of self-confidence, peer pressure).

WHAT YOU NEED
Construction paper (black, brown, and white)
Scissors
Black marker
Figure of a preteen boy from page 155

WHAT YOU DO

1. Cut letters for the caption from black paper and mount them on the board as shown.

2. Cut a winding path with side roads from brown paper. Label the main path "The Christian Life." Mount it on the board.

3. Cut signs from white paper and signposts from brown paper. Print words of warning on the signs and place them along the side roads on the board.

4. Attach the figure of the boy to the beginning of the path.

WHAT YOU TALK ABOUT
Ask students what kinds of detours the devil may try to tempt them to go down in their Christian lives. Discuss the way to keep from giving in and following these side roads. Talk about the importance of daily prayer and Bible study.

WHAT YOU NEED

Construction paper (red, blue, green, yellow, white, and gray)

Scissors

Colored markers

String

Figure of boy from page 155

WHAT YOU DO

1. Cut letters for the caption from red paper and mount them across the top of the board.

2. Cut a strip of blue paper with a wavy top to represent water. Print Hebrews 10:23 on the water as shown. Mount the water on the board.

3. Cut a shark from gray paper, enlarging the pattern from the board. Mount the shark on the board.

4. Enlarge the figure of the boy on white paper, color it, and cut it out. Attach it to the center of the board.

5. Cut several circles from colored paper to represent balloons. Have students write some of God's promises on the balloons and attach them to the board.

6. Cut short lengths of string to attach the balloons to the boy's hands.

WHAT YOU TALK ABOUT

Discuss God's promises. Have students share their favorite ones, then have them use their Bibles to find additional promises. Discuss how God has kept the promises on the board.

God's Gifts to Me

Answered Prayer

His Love

My Life

My Love

My Praise

Salvation

My Gifts to God

WHAT YOU NEED
- Construction paper (red and white)
- Scissors
- Gift wrap and ribbon
- Manger scene (from a Christmas card)
- Glue
- Colored markers

WHAT YOU DO

1 Cut letters for the caption from red paper and mount them at the top and bottom of the board as shown.

2 Glue the manger scene to a sheet of white paper. Mount it on the board. Cut a piece of gift wrap the same size as the paper. Glue a ribbon bow on it. Mount the gift wrap over the top of the manger scene. Attach it to the board at the top only so it can be lifted up to see the scene underneath.

3 Hand out white paper of various sizes and colored markers. Have students draw pictures or write words to indicate gifts God has given them or gifts they have given God. Let them choose gift wrap and ribbon to cover their papers; then mount them all on the board as you did the manger scene.

WHAT YOU TALK ABOUT

Talk about the gift of God's Son coming to earth for us. Then discuss each of the other gifts on the board that God has given us. Discuss what we can give to God. Talk about each gift to God on the board.

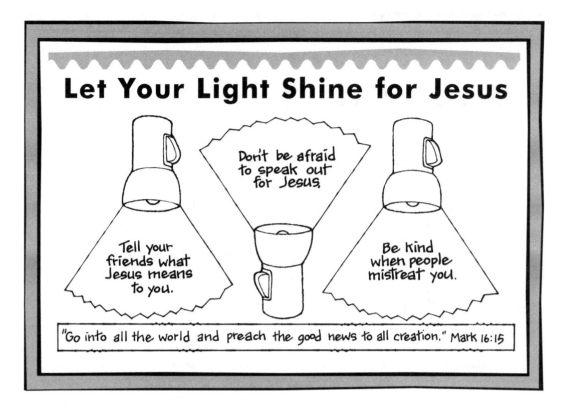

WHAT YOU NEED

Construction paper (brown or gray
and yellow
Scissors
Black marker

WHAT YOU DO

1. Cut letters for the caption from yellow paper and mount them at the top of the board.

2. Print Mark 16:15 on a strip of yellow paper and mount it across the bottom of the board.

3. Cut large flashlights from brown or gray paper and cut the light for the flashlights from yellow paper as shown. Print on the yellow flashlight beams some ways to shine for Jesus (see the sample). Mount the flashlights and beams on the board as shown.

WHAT YOU TALK ABOUT

Talk about some specific things students can do to shine for Jesus. Challenge them to put these ideas into practice. Ask them what they think the results would be if every Christian would shine for Jesus every day.

Right or Wrong? It's Your Choice!

WHAT YOU NEED
- Construction paper (dark and light green)
- Scissors
- Question mark patterns (enlarged from the board)
- Black markers or pens

WHAT YOU DO

1 Cut letters for the caption from dark green paper and mount them on the board.

2 Cut a large question mark from light green paper for each student. Hand out the question marks and black markers or pens. Have students print choices they face each day on the question marks. Mount the question marks on the board. OPTION: If you are using the board throughout a unit on choices, make exclamation points. Each week, as you study scriptural guidelines for making right choices, have students print them on the exclamation points and add them to the board.

WHAT YOU TALK ABOUT
Ask students to share some of the choices they face every day (to lie or tell the truth, to go along with the crowd and do wrong or stand alone and do right, to witness for Jesus or not say anything, and so on). Explain that if we depend on the Lord, He will give us the wisdom and courage to choose right instead of wrong.

WHAT YOU NEED

- Construction paper (a variety of colors)
- Scissors
- Black marker
- Figure of Jesus from page 144
- String
- Confetti
- Glue
- Real balloons (optional)

WHAT YOU DO

1. Print the caption on a bright colored strip of paper with wavy edges and mount it at the top of the board.

2. Mount the figure of Jesus on the board.

3. Print the reasons to celebrate Jesus on colored strips of paper. Mount them all over the board.

4. Cut circles from colored paper to represent balloons or blow up real balloons and attach them to the board as shown.

5. Attach string to the balloons, gather the strings together near the end, and attach them to the board.

6. Use a tiny bit of glue to attach confetti to the board for a festive look.

WHAT YOU TALK ABOUT

Discuss some of the exciting reasons to celebrate Jesus (His death for our sins, His resurrection, His love and forgiveness for us, and so on). Ask students to share some of the ways we can show that we celebrate Jesus.

KEEP ON PRAYING

Sun	Mon	Tues	Wed	Thurs	Fri	Sat

"Be joyful always; pray continually; give thanks in all circumstances, for this is God's will for you in Christ Jesus." 1 Thessalonians 5:16-18

WHAT YOU NEED

Construction paper (purple and lavender)
Scissors
Fine tip black marker
Large calendar page (for one week or one month)

WHAT YOU DO

1. Cut letters for the caption from purple paper and mount them across the top of the board.

2. Use the illustration as a guide to cut praying hands out of lavender paper. Print 1 Thessalonians 5:16-18 on the hands and attach them to the board.

3. Mount the calendar page on the board.

4. Ask students to share praise prayers, thank-You prayers, and prayer requests. Print a prayer on each day of the week on the calendar.

WHAT YOU TALK ABOUT

Ask students how often they feel the need to pray. Discuss how daily prayer can make a difference in our attitudes, in our relationship with the Lord, and in what happens in our lives. Have a prayer time, using some of the statements on the prayer calendar.

WHAT YOU NEED

- Blue construction paper
- Black and red markers
- Fine tip markers or pens
- Colored index cards

WHAT YOU DO

1. Print the caption on blue paper and mount it on the left side of the board. (Be sure to make the first letter of each word bigger and bolder than the others.)

2. Print Ephesians 5:1 on blue paper and mount it under the caption.

3. Hand out index cards and markers or pens. Have students write on the cards "sticky situations" they have faced and the choices they had (using the format shown above). Mount the cards on the board.

4. Use a red marker to check on each card what Jesus would do in that situation.

WHAT YOU TALK ABOUT

Discuss what Jesus would do if He were physically with students as they live with their families, go to school, participate in various activities, and so on. Ask students to share "sticky situations" they've experienced. Discuss what Jesus would do in each situation. Point out that Jesus may not be with us physically, but He is definitely with Christians through His Holy Spirit. Asking ourselves what He would do is a good way to decide what we should do.

God Wants You

"whatever you do, work at
it with all your heart,
as working for the Lord,
not for men."
Colossians 3:23

to Be the Best You Can Be

WHAT YOU NEED
- White paper
- Construction paper (red and blue)
- Scissors
- Black marker
- Glove stuffed with fabric or tissues
- Stapler and staples

WHAT YOU DO

1. Cover the board with white paper.

2. Cut letters for the caption from blue paper and mount them on the covered board as shown.

3. Print Colossians 3:23 on the left side of the white paper background.

4. Cut a large heart out of red paper and attach it to the right side of the board.

5. Manipulate the stuffed glove so that the index finger is pointing out and the other fingers are bent. Staple them to the palm of the glove to hold them. Attach the glove to the center of the heart so the finger is pointing out.

WHAT YOU TALK ABOUT
Discuss why God wants us to do our best. Ask students why God deserves our best. What difference can it make in the way we do things if we're doing them for the Lord instead of doing them for other people? Talk about the importance of doing our best in small jobs as well as big ones.

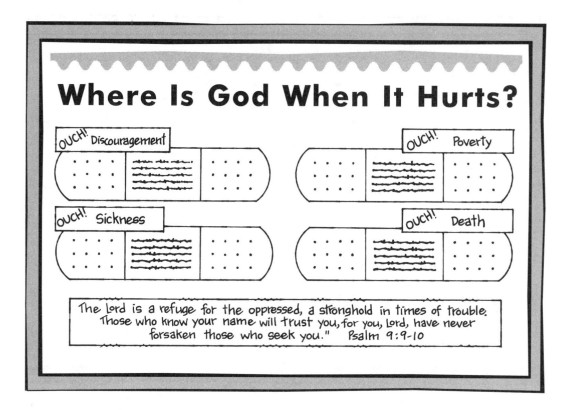

WHAT YOU NEED

Construction paper (red and tan or
cream)
Scissors
Black marker
Adhesive bandage (optional)

WHAT YOU TALK ABOUT

Ask students to share some problems they have
experienced or have seen others experience. Ask
them how they think the Lord can help with
these problems. Read the Bible verses on the
board and look up other verses of comfort as
necessary, using a concordance.

WHAT YOU DO

1 Cut letters for the caption from red paper and mount them
at the top of the board.

2 Print Psalm 9:9, 10 on a strip of tan or cream paper and
attach it to the bottom of the board.

3 Cut word strips from red paper to be "OUCH!" labels. Print
on them some problems God helps us face. (See the board
illustration for ideas.)

4 Cut large bandage shapes from tan or cream paper as shown
above. Use a black marker to make the dots. Print on the
bandages Bible verses that show how God helps us with each
of the problems on the "OUCH!" labels. Suggested verses
follow. Death: "For as in Adam all die, so in Christ all will be
made alive" (1 Corinthians 15:22). Discouragement: "Do not
be discouraged, for the Lord your God will be with you
wherever you go" (Joshua 1:9). Poverty: "He will respond to
the prayer of the destitute; He will not despise their plea"
(Psalm 102:17). Sickness: "The Lord will sustain him on his
sickbed and restore him from his bed of illness" (Psalm 41:3).

5 Attach the "OUCH!" labels and bandage shapes to the board.
Attach real bandages on the board if desired.

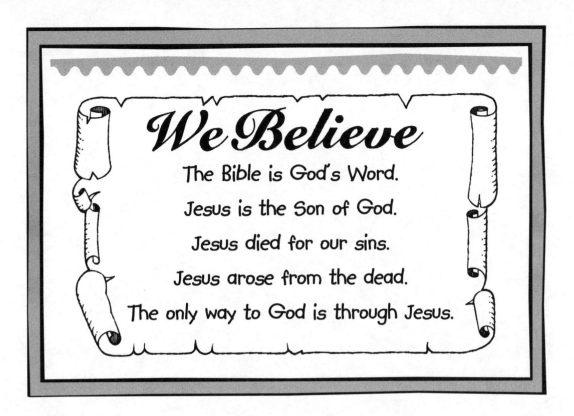

We Believe

The Bible is God's Word.

Jesus is the Son of God.

Jesus died for our sins.

Jesus arose from the dead.

The only way to God is through Jesus.

WHAT YOU NEED
White paper
Scissors
Black marker

WHAT YOU DO

1. Cut a large piece of paper to look like an old parchment document. (Curl the corners around a pencil.)

2. Use fancy script lettering to print the caption at the top of the paper as shown.

3. Ask students to help you come up with a list of the basic beliefs of your church. Print the list on a large piece of white paper.

4. Mount the paper on the board.

WHAT YOU TALK ABOUT
Ask students where the church's beliefs come from. Help them find Scripture verses that support the items mentioned on the board. Some possible Scriptures might include Matthew 28:18-20; John 14:6; Acts 2:38; Acts 4:12; 1 Corinthians 15:3, 4; 2 Timothy 3:16; Hebrews 4:12.

seasonal Bulletin Boards

Use the bulletin boards on the following pages to focus attention on the seasons of the year. These not only will be colorful focal points, they will also help children learn important truths. Young children can learn that they should be thankful to God for the wonderful variety of weather and natural displays that He provides throughout the year. Though some may live in areas where the seasonal changes are less obvious, they can still relate to the idea of snow and falling leaves. Be sure to use some natural items on these boards whenever possible for added interest.

Older children can think about the seasons in greater depth, discovering how they can respond to God in various ways, depending on the time of year. For example, in spring when people are busy getting houses cleaned, yards mowed or raked, and gardens prepared, older children will find many opportunities to apply what they have learned in God's Word about helping others and serving Him.

Adults too will appreciate the emphasis of these seasonal bulletin boards. Try to put them in areas where they can be seen, or be sure to let the children's parents know that they are welcome to visit to see the boards.

Whenever possible, let the children be the ones to provide the extra items to go on the bulletin boards (vacation items, spring items, autumn leaves, and so on). You may want to send a short note home to parents to let them know what their children have volunteered to bring for the boards. Let them know that the items will need to stay at the church for awhile until the bulletin board is changed.

WHAT YOU NEED

Construction paper (red and white)
Scissors
Colored markers
Pictures of drawings of seasonal things
  (seeds, flowers, vegetables, sun, moon
  and stars, rain, and snow)
Seasonal items (sunglasses, mittens,
  pictures of rainboots and umbrella)

WHAT YOU DO

1. Cut letters for the caption from red construction paper and mount them at the top and bottom of the board.

2. Draw a large rainbow across the board as a background. Or cut out colored strips of paper and attach them to the board to make a rainbow.

3. Copy the Bible verse, Genesis 8:22, on a white sheet of paper and attach it to the center of the board.

4. Surround the Scripture with seasonal pictures and items.

WHAT YOU TALK ABOUT

Have a volunteer read the Bible verse. Talk about the events surrounding God's promise (the flood and Noah and his family being spared). Talk about God's faithfulness in making the seasons continue to follow one another every year.

WHAT YOU NEED

Flowered gift wrap
Construction paper (dark green, light green, white or yellow)
Scissors
Black fine-tip marker
Plastic or paper spring flowers

WHAT YOU DO

1. Cover the board with flowered gift wrap.

2. Cut letters for the caption from dark green paper and mount them on the board as shown.

3. Copy the poem on light green paper and attach it to the center of the board.

4. Ask students to name jobs they can do to help others this spring. Print the jobs on small pieces of white or yellow paper and scatter them over the board.

5. Scatter plastic or paper spring flowers over the board.

WHAT YOU TALK ABOUT

Discuss various ways children can serve the Lord by doing practical, everyday jobs for their parents and other people. Discuss each of the jobs on the board. Encourage children to ask their parents for permission to sign up and do the jobs. (You may want to ask people in the church to suggest jobs they would like to have done and put them on the board.)

Welcome, Spring

"See the winter is past; the rains are over and gone; Flowers appear on the earth; the season for singing has come, the cooing of doves is heard in our land." Song of Song's 2:11-12

WHAT YOU NEED

Construction paper (pink, yellow, light blue)
Scissors
Black marker
Photos or real samples of spring items (flowers, leaves, bird feathers, maple leaves, and so on)

WHAT YOU DO

1 Cut letters for the caption from pink construction paper and mount them across the top of the board.

2 Print the Bible verses, Song of Songs 2:11, 12, on a piece of light blue paper and attach it at the bottom of the board.

3 Fill the board with spring things. Begin by cutting a large sun from yellow paper and mounting it in a corner of the board.

WHAT YOU TALK ABOUT

Discuss the spring items on the board and read the Bible verses. Ask children what they like most about spring.

WHAT YOU NEED

Construction paper (purple, brown, dark blue)

Scissors

Summer vacation items (sunglasses, camping equipment, swim fins, sun visor, and so on)

Suitcase pattern from page 157

WHAT YOU DO

1. Cut letters for the caption from purple construction paper and mount them on the bulletin board as shown.

2. Enlarge the suitcase pattern and cut it out of brown paper. Mount it on the board.

3. Cut a Bible from dark blue paper and print BIBLE on the front. Attach it to the board on top of the suitcase.

4. Let the children attach the summer vacation items around the suitcase.

WHAT YOU TALK ABOUT

Ask children where they'll be going for summer vacation. Ask them if we can go on vacation from God. How can they take God with them wherever they go? (Taking their Bibles to read and being sure to pray every day.)

Summer Is a Growing Time

How can you grow as a Christian this summer?

Growing Tips
1. Read your Bible
2. Memorize Bible verses
3. Pray
4. Come to Sunday School and church

"We ought always to thank God ... because your faith is growing more and more and the love everyone of you has for each other is increasing." 2 Thessalonians 1:3

WHAT YOU NEED
Construction paper (green, yellow, white)
Scissors
Colored markers
Pattern of a child and corn from page 156 and of a cornstalk from page 157

WHAT YOU DO

1. Cut the letters for the caption from green paper and mount them across the top of the board.

2. Using the patterns, cut corn stalks from green paper and add ears of corn cut from yellow paper. Mount the plants on the left side of the board.

3. Enlarge the pattern of the child on white paper and cut it out. Use markers to color clothes and add features. Attach the child next to the corn stalks.

4. Print the question and the growing tips on a piece of white paper. Attach it to the right side of the board.

5. Print 2 Thessalonians 1:3 on a yellow strip of paper and mount it under the corn stalks and child.

WHAT YOU TALK ABOUT
Ask the children who have gardens if they have noticed things growing. Point out that we plant most things in the spring and they grow during the warm summer months. Explain that God wants us to grow as Christians in the summer and all the rest of the year too. Ask children to suggest other things they can do to help them grow.

As the leaves fall from the trees Lord, I fall down on my knees, To praise You!

WHAT YOU NEED

Construction paper (orange, yellow, red, brown)
White paper
Scissors
Pattern of praying child from page 152
Glue
Pencils
Black marker
Real autumn leaves

WHAT YOU DO

1. Cut letters for the caption from orange paper and attach them to the board.

2. Enlarge the pattern of the praying child and cut it from brown paper.

3. Print the prayer poem on white paper and glue it to the praying child silhouette. Mount it on the board.

4. Hand out construction paper, pencils, and scissors. Have children cut out autumn leaves of a variety of kinds and colors. (You may want to enlarge the leaves above for patterns.) Attach the leaves all over the board. Add some real leaves to add interest.

WHAT YOU TALK ABOUT

Ask children what it means to fall before God. Explain that we don't have to bow down to pray, but bowing shows reverence for God. Discuss some of the things the children want to pray about.

AS WHITE AS SNOW

"'Come now, let us reason together, says the Lord. Though your sins are like scarlet, they shall be white as snow.'" Isaiah 1:18a

WHAT YOU NEED

Dark blue paper
White paper
Scissors
Dark blue marker
Cotton

WHAT YOU DO

1. Cover the board with dark blue paper.

2. Cut letters for the caption from white paper and mount them at the top of the board.

3. Print Isaiah 1:18a on white paper and mount it at the center of the board. Attach cotton around the Bible verse for a snowy border.

4. Hand out white paper and scissors. Show children how to fold and cut the paper to make snowflakes. (a. Cut paper into a square. b. Fold it into smaller and smaller triangles. c. Cut small sections out and round off the corners. d. Unfold the paper.)

5. Attach the snowflakes all over the board.

WHAT YOU TALK ABOUT

Read the Bible verse and ask children to explain what they think it means. Point out to them that snow helps remind us of God's forgiveness and love.

Holiday Bulletin Boards

The major holidays covered by the bulletin boards on the following pages are not all religious holidays, but they are ones that will probably be recognized, to some extent, by most churches. Some of the topics may correlate with lessons you are teaching. If so, make the board a part of the lesson. Discuss it and weave it into your teaching. If, however, a bulletin board does not correlate with any of your lessons, you may want to set aside a special time immediately before or on the actual holiday to draw children's attention to the board and discuss it.

The boards are provided in chronological order, beginning with New Year's and ending with Christmas. Whenever possible, involve your children in assembling the board as well as discussing the lesson it teaches or the truth it illustrates.

Be sure to put each board up well in advance of the holiday it focuses on. Since children are often absent from church during holidays, you'll want to make sure it's available before and/or after the actual holiday.

Many of these bulletin boards are interactive, involving children in participating in the creation of the boards as well as responding to them in some way. If possible, think of ways to involve the children in the non-interactive boards.

HOW TO HAVE A HAPPY NEW YEAR

"Trust in the Lord with all your heart and lean not on your own understanding; in all your ways acknowledge him, and he will make your paths straight."

Proverbs 3: 5-6

WHAT YOU NEED

Gold or silver paper
Construction paper (red, white, blue)
Scissors
Black marker
New year celebration items
   (noisemakers, confetti, small calendar,
   and so on)

WHAT YOU DO

1. Cover the board with gold or silver paper.

2. Cut letters for the caption from red paper and mount them across the top of the board.

3. Draw a large open Bible shape on blue paper and cut it out. Cut the same shape a little smaller from white paper. Print Proverbs 3:5, 6 on the white paper. Glue it to the blue paper and mount it on the board.

4. Surround the verses with New Year celebration items.

WHAT YOU TALK ABOUT

Read the Bible verses aloud. Ask children how they think obeying these verses can help them have a happy New Year. Talk about specific ways they can obey the verses.

Love the World Through Me, Lord

Read to my sister

Visit my grandmother

Obey my mom and dad

"Dear friends, let us love one another, for love comes from God. Everyone who loves has been born of God and knows God" I John 4:7

WHAT YOU NEED
Red paper
White construction paper
Scissors
White index cards
Heart stickers
Black fine tip markers or pens

WHAT YOU DO

1. Cover the board with red paper.

2. Cut letters for the caption from white paper and mount them at the top of the board.

3. Print the Bible verse, I John 4:7, on a strip of white paper and attach it to the bottom of the board.

4. Place a heart sticker in the corner of each index card. Hand out the cards and pens or markers. Have children write on the cards how and to whom they will show God's love. These should be practical things that they can do on their own. Scatter the cards all over the board.

WHAT YOU TALK ABOUT
Before the children put their cards on the board, discuss them. Some children may need help in thinking of someone to help or something to do. Suggest ideas such as reading to a little sister, visiting a grandparent in a nursing home, obeying parents without complaining, inviting a neighbor over to play, being kind to someone who makes fun of me. Challenge the children to actually perform the tasks they wrote down this week.

WHAT YOU NEED

Construction paper (light green, gray, white, yellow)
Scissors
Easter lily pattern from page 154
Black markers or pens

WHAT YOU TALK ABOUT

Talk about Easter. Ask children to explain why we celebrate it. Why is it such an important day for Christians? Take a minute to let volunteers pray, praising God for Easter.

WHAT YOU DO

1. Cut letters for the caption from light green paper and mount them at the top of the board.

2. Cut a strip of green paper to represent grass and attach it to the bottom of the board.

3. Cut a large sun from yellow paper and mount it on the board.

4. Cut an open tomb and stone from gray paper and mount it at the center of the board. (Use yellow paper behind the door of the tomb to look like light coming out of it.) Print on the tombstone "The tomb was empty."

5. Make copies of the Easter lily pattern for the children to trace. Hand out the patterns, white and green paper, scissors, and markers or pens. Have the children cut lilies from white paper and make stems and leaves from green paper. Ask each child to write on a lily why Easter is special to him or her.

6. Let the children attach their lilies (with stems and leaves) to the board as shown.

WHAT YOU NEED

Construction paper (purple, lavender,
    white)
Scissors
Colored markers
Photos of children's moms

WHAT YOU DO

1. Cut letters for the caption from purple paper and mount them across the top of the board.

2. Print the poem on a sheet of lavender paper and mount it at the center of the board.

3. Hand out small slips of white paper and markers. Have each child finish this sentence: I love my mom because . . . .

4. Mount the photos of mothers all over the board with the children's cards under them.

WHAT YOU TALK ABOUT

Ask children to share stories to explain why they love their moms. Discuss ways the children can honor and show love to their mothers today. Take a minute to thank God for each mom.

WHAT YOU NEED

Construction paper (red, white, blue)
Photographs and stories of men and
   women who died in American wars
Red marker
Gold or silver star stickers

WHAT YOU DO

1. Print the caption, using a red marker, on white paper. Add star stickers around the caption and mount it at the top of the board.

2. Ask people in your church for stories and photographs of men and women who died in American wars. Mount the stories and photos on red, white, and blue paper and mount them on the board.

WHAT YOU TALK ABOUT

Ask the children if they know of anyone in their families who died in war. Ask them why people are willing to give their lives in battle. Point out that we owe our freedom to thousands of people who fought for this country and died. Explain that the purpose of Memorial Day is to remember and honor these people.

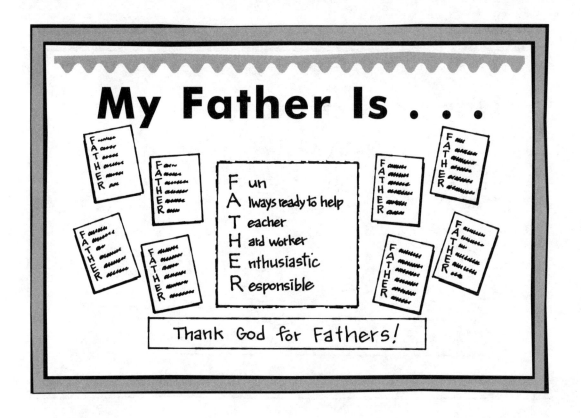

WHAT YOU NEED

- Construction paper (light brown and orange)
- White paper
- Scissors
- Black markers
- Pencils

WHAT YOU DO

1. Cut letters for the caption from orange paper and mount them at the top of the board.

2. Print "Thank God for Fathers" on a strip of orange paper and attach it to the bottom of the board.

3. Print the acrostic on a sheet of light brown paper and attach it to the center of the board.

4. Hand out white paper, pencils, and markers. Have children come up with their own acrostics to describe their fathers. (Have them work with pencil first; then go over the final acrostic with black marker.) Mount the children's acrostics on the board.

WHAT YOU TALK ABOUT

Ask children to talk about their fathers, describing them and telling what they enjoy doing and what makes them special. Take time to pray together, thanking God for each father.

WHAT YOU NEED

- Red paper
- Construction paper (dark blue and white)
- Scissors
- Colored markers
- String
- Glue
- Gold or silver star stickers
- Candle pattern from page 153

WHAT YOU DO

1. Cover the board with red paper.

2. Cut letters for the caption from dark blue paper and mount them on the board.

3. Using a red marker, print Psalm 33:12a on a strip of white paper and attach it to the bottom of the board.

4. Cut a birthday cake from white paper. Print on it the number of years old the U.S.A. is. Attach the cake to the board.

5. Make several copies of the candle pattern. Hand out scissors, candle patterns, string, glue, and markers. Let the children color and cut out candles and put them on the cake. (Glue string to the candles for wicks.)

6. Add star stickers all over the board.

WHAT YOU TALK ABOUT

Ask children to explain what Americans celebrate on July 4th. Ask them to share why they think America is the best country in which to live. Pray, thanking God for the U.S.A.

WHAT YOU NEED

Construction paper (red, yellow)
Scissors
White paper
Crayons
Black markers or pens
Turkey pattern from page 156

WHAT YOU DO

1. Cut letters for the caption from red paper and mount them across the top of the board.

2. Print Psalm 95:2a on a sheet of yellow paper and attach it to the board.

3. Enlarge the turkey pattern and make a copy for every child.

4. Hand out turkeys, white paper, scissors, and crayons. Have each child write a prayer of thanks to God on a turkey. Then they may color the turkeys, cut them out and attach them to the board.

WHAT YOU TALK ABOUT

Ask students what they are thankful for. Spend a few minutes brainstorming ideas. After they have written their prayers for the bulletin board, take time to have students pray their prayers aloud.

BIRTH ANNOUNCEMENT

Name — Jesus
Birthplace — Bethlehem stable
Time — When the fullness of time was come
Parents — Mary and God the Father
Birth Attendants — sheep, cow, donkey

"Today in the town of David a Savior has been born to you; he is Christ the Lord," Luke 2:11

WHAT YOU NEED
- Construction paper (light blue)
- White paper
- Scissors
- Colored markers
- Picture of Baby Jesus in the manger from page 150
- Figure of angel from page 154
- Baby items (rattles, booties, teething rings, pacifiers, and so on)

WHAT YOU DO

1. Cut letters for the caption from light blue paper and mount them at the top of the board.

2. Glue a picture of Baby Jesus in the manger on the left side of a large sheet of white paper. Under the picture print Luke 2:11. On the right side of the white paper print the birth information shown on the board. Mount the white paper on the board.

3. Cut out angels and attach them to the top corners of the white paper.

4. Decorate the rest of the board with baby rattles, booties, and other baby items.

WHAT YOU TALK ABOUT
Ask children how Jesus' birth was announced. Was a card sent? Who were the first to hear of His birth? How did we hear about His birth?

Children's Ministry Bulletin Boards

Every church has special occasions, meetings, signup campaigns, and other events that need to be publicized throughout the year. What better way to make important events known and emphasize specific themes and topics than bulletin boards! The bulletin boards on the following pages use eye-catching visuals, bright colors, Bible verses, and even humor to get the point across. Children will enjoy helping you put them together whenever possible.

Adapt the ideas to your own needs. And remember, don't leave any bulletin board up for too long or it will lose its impact. If the board is left up for over a month, people will not even notice it anymore. Keep their interest by changing the bulletin board frequently.

You don't have to be an artist to use these boards. If you have a large Christian education file full of pictures and figures and letters, that's great. If you don't, you can usually just use a copier to enlarge the figures from the illustrations of the bulletin boards.

Most of the bulletin boards in this book use cut-out letters rather than hand lettering for the main captions. That's because few of us have handwriting that is neat enough and also bold enough to capture attention. Large colorful letters are needed to immediately communicate the theme of the board. Always make everything on the board as large as possible so that a person need only glance at it to be hit with a message. Hopefully, the board will entice the person to come closer to read the smaller print on the board.

Providing quality bulletin boards with important messages is a real ministry in the church. It takes a commitment of time that many people are unwilling to make. People may not think to thank you for your bulletin board ministry, but you can be sure that they're glad you do it.

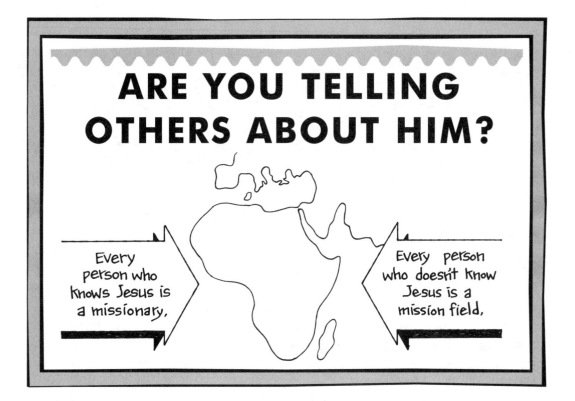

ARE YOU TELLING OTHERS ABOUT HIM?

Every person who knows Jesus is a missionary,

Every person who doesn't know Jesus is a mission field,

WHAT YOU NEED

Large world map
Light blue and dark blue paper
Dark blue marker
Scissors

WHAT YOU DO

1 Cover the bulletin board with the world map. (If you don't have a map big enough, sketch the continents on a large sheet of white paper to use as a background.)

2 Cut letters for the caption from dark blue paper. Mount them at the center of the board as shown above.

3 Print the two statements ("Every person who knows Jesus is a missionary." "Every person who doesn't know Jesus is a mission field.") on light blue paper and mount them on the board.
OPTION: Replace the statements with pictures and information about missionaries your church supports. Include suggestions of ways members can help, such as items they can donate or specific prayer requests.

WHAT YOU NEED
Red construction paper
White paper
Scissors
Black marker
Food containers (bread wrapper, cereal box, milk carton, and so on)

WHAT YOU DO

1. Cut letters for the caption from red paper and mount them on the board.

2. Print the Bible verse, Proverbs 14:21b, on white paper. Mount the verse on the board on a sheet of red paper.

3. Print the food pantry directions on white paper, such as specific items the pantry is collecting. Mount them on the board on a sheet of red paper.

4. Attach food wrappers and containers all over the board.

Get on Track— Memorize God's Word

BIBLE MEMORY LINE

John 3:16

Jeremiah 31:3

Proverbs 3:5

1 John 1:9

Romans 5:8

Titus 3:5

Psalm 23:1

Matthew 5:16

Hebrews 4:12

WHAT YOU NEED

Construction paper (red and black)
Scissors
Train engine and car pattern from
    page 152
Black markers
Small strips of paper

WHAT YOU DO

1. Cut letters for the caption from black construction paper and mount them on the board.

2. Enlarge the train engine pattern and cut it from red paper. Mount it on the board as shown.

3. Enlarge the box car pattern and make several copies on red paper. Print on each car the reference of a Bible memory verse. Mount the cars on the board, connecting them with small red strips of paper.

4. As children memorize the Bible verses, let each print his or her name on a slip of paper and place it in the appropriate box car.

WHAT YOU NEED

Construction paper (black, yellow)
Scissors
Red marker
Sheet music
Photo of children's choir or choirs

WHAT YOU DO

1. Cut letters for the caption from black paper and mount them at the top of the board. (Cut the two U's from yellow paper so they stand out.)

2. Attach sheet music to the rest of the board. (The other items on the board will cover some of the music.)

3. Print Psalm 69:30a on yellow paper and attach it to the board.

4. Print "Choir Signup Sheet" on yellow paper and attach it to the board.

5. Mount a photo of the children's choir(s) on the board.

6. Cut music notes and symbols from black paper and scatter them over the board.

Ready-Set-Go Back to School

"The Lord himself goes before you and will be with you."

Deuteronomy 31:8a

A brand new school year can be scary it's true. But open the door To see who'll go with you.

WHAT YOU NEED

- Yellow construction paper
- Scissors
- Black marker
- Picture of Jesus from page 145
- Photos of children (optional)

WHAT YOU DO

1. Cut letters for the caption from yellow construction paper and mount them on the bulletin board as shown.

2. Enlarge the school bus from the board and cut it out of yellow paper. Use a black marker to draw windows and a door. Cut the door out on three sides. Fold it on the left side so it can be opened and closed.

3. Print the poem on the side of the bus and mount it on the board.

4. Print the verse, Deuteronomy 31:8a, on a small piece of paper. Place the verse and the picture of Jesus behind the bus door.

5. Draw happy faces in the bus windows or attach photos of your children.

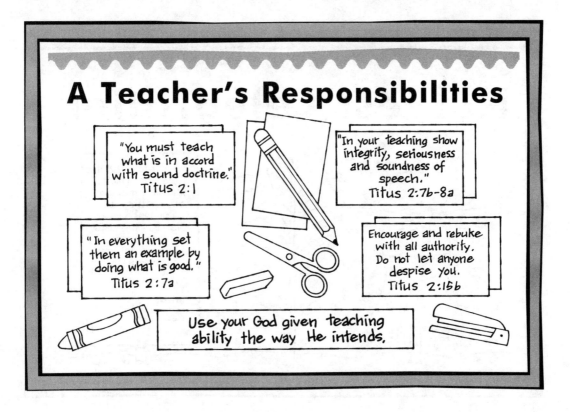

A Teacher's Responsibilities

"You must teach what is in accord with sound doctrine."
Titus 2:1

"In your teaching show integrity, seriousness and soundness of speech."
Titus 2:7b-8a

"In everything set them an example by doing what is good."
Titus 2:7a

Encourage and rebuke with all authority. Do not let anyone despise you.
Titus 2:15b

Use your God given teaching ability the way He intends.

WHAT YOU NEED
Black construction paper
White paper
Scissors
Fine tip black marker
Red marker
Sunday School supplies (pencils, erasers, paper, Bible, student worksheets)

WHAT YOU DO

1. Cut the letters for the caption from black paper and mount them across the top of the board.

2. Use a red marker to print the sentence on a strip of white paper and mount it at the bottom of the board.

3. Using a black marker, print Bible verses Titus 2:1, 7a, 7b-8a, and 15b on individual pieces of paper. Use a red marker to check each verse. Mount the verses on the board.

4. Attach Sunday school supplies around the board.

Harvest Celebration

The garden and the fields are brown;
All growing things are settling down.
The Lord has blessed - the crops were great
And now its time to celebrate!

Date:

Time:

Place:

WHAT YOU NEED

Construction paper (green, yellow, white, black)
Scissors
Figures of scarecrow, corn, crows, and cornstalk from pages 154, 156, and 157
Colored markers
Real hay or straw and kernels of corn
Glue

WHAT YOU DO

1. Cut letters for the caption from green paper and attach them across the top of the board.

2. Enlarge the pattern of the scarecrow and color it. Attach it to the left side of the board. Glue some real straw or hay on the scarecrow.

3. Enlarge the pattern of the crows on black paper and attach them to the board.

4. Cut a corn stalk from green paper and glue on it ears of corn made from yellow paper. Attach the corn stalk to the board.

5. Print the poem on white paper. Add information about the harvest celebration (date, time, place) and mount the paper on the board.

6. Glue a few kernels of corn and some wisps of straw or hay to the board.

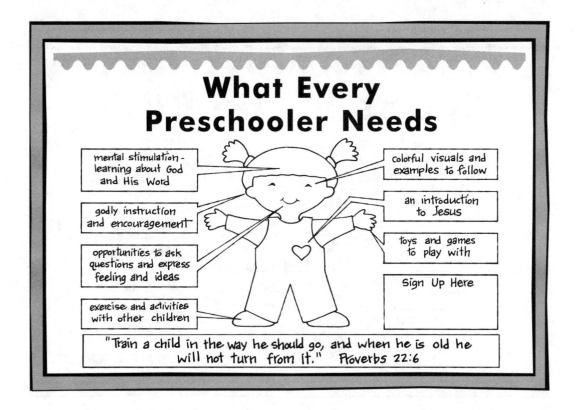

WHAT YOU NEED

Construction paper (orange and white)
Scissors
Figure of a preschooler from page 156
Colored markers
Orange yarn

WHAT YOU DO

1. Cut letters for the caption from orange paper and mount them at the top of the board.

2. Enlarge the figure of the preschooler on white paper, color it, and cut it out. Mount it on the board.

3. Print the explanations on white paper and attach them to the board. Connect them to the appropriate places on the preschooler with orange yarn.

4. Print the Bible verse, Proverbs 22:6, on orange paper and attach it to the bottom of the board.

5. Attach a signup sheet (for teachers, supplies, or toy donations, and so on) and necessary information on the board.

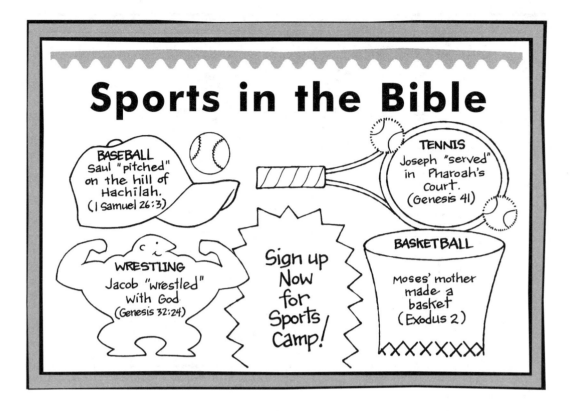

WHAT YOU NEED

Sports pages from newspapers
Construction paper (red, white)
Scissors
Colored markers

WHAT YOU DO

1. Cover the board with newspaper sports pages.

2. Cut letters for the caption from red paper and attach them across the top of the board.

3. Print the four descriptions of Bible sports on three separate sheets of white paper. Draw a small symbol of the sport next to each one. Attach the descriptions to the board.

4. Attach a signup sheet in the middle of the board.

WHAT YOU NEED

Construction paper (black, tan, pink)
Scissors
Black fine tip marker
Figure of Jesus with children from
    page 155

WHAT YOU DO

1. Cut letters for the caption from black paper and mount them at the top of the board.

2. Mount the figure of Jesus and the children at the center of the board.

3. Print the directions on a strip of pink or tan paper and attach it to the board under the caption.

4. Print Matthew 19:13a on a strip of pink or tan paper and attach it to the bottom of the board.

5. Cut handprint shapes from pink and tan paper. Print on each one the name of a child (and a prayer request for that child if you like). Mount the handprints all over the board. Encourage people to take them home and pray for the children.

WHAT YOU NEED

White paper
Construction paper (dark blue)
Scissors
Colored markers
Photo of person being spotlighted

WHAT YOU DO

1. Cover the board with white paper.

2. Draw two spotlights in the bottom corners of the paper with light shining toward the center of the board.

3. Cut letters for the caption from dark blue paper and mount them across the top of the board.

4. Print the Bible verses, 1 Thessalonians 5:12-13a, at the bottom of the paper.

5. Mount a sheet of dark blue paper in the center of the board for a frame. Attach the photo of the person being spotlighted on the frame with the person's name and a description of that person's ministry.

God Wants You in Children's Ministry!

Job Pool

Dive in today and get in the swim of things!

WHAT YOU NEED

- Construction paper (blue, white)
- Scissors
- Figure of a person diving from page 155
- Colored markers

WHAT YOU DO

1. Cut letters for the caption from blue paper and mount them at the top of the board.

2. Cut a large oval from blue paper. Draw wavy lines on it to make it look like water. Mount it on the board.

3. Use the pattern to draw a person diving off of a diving board. Color and cut the figure out and place it over the water.

4. Print the instructions on a strip of white paper and attach it beneath the pool.

5. Print the "Job Pool" on the water, listing opportunities in children's ministries.

144

Patterns for pages 12, 26, 51, 65, 68, 90, 136

145

146

Patterns for pages 36, 64

Patterns for pages 10, 16

147

148

Patterns for pages 10, 30

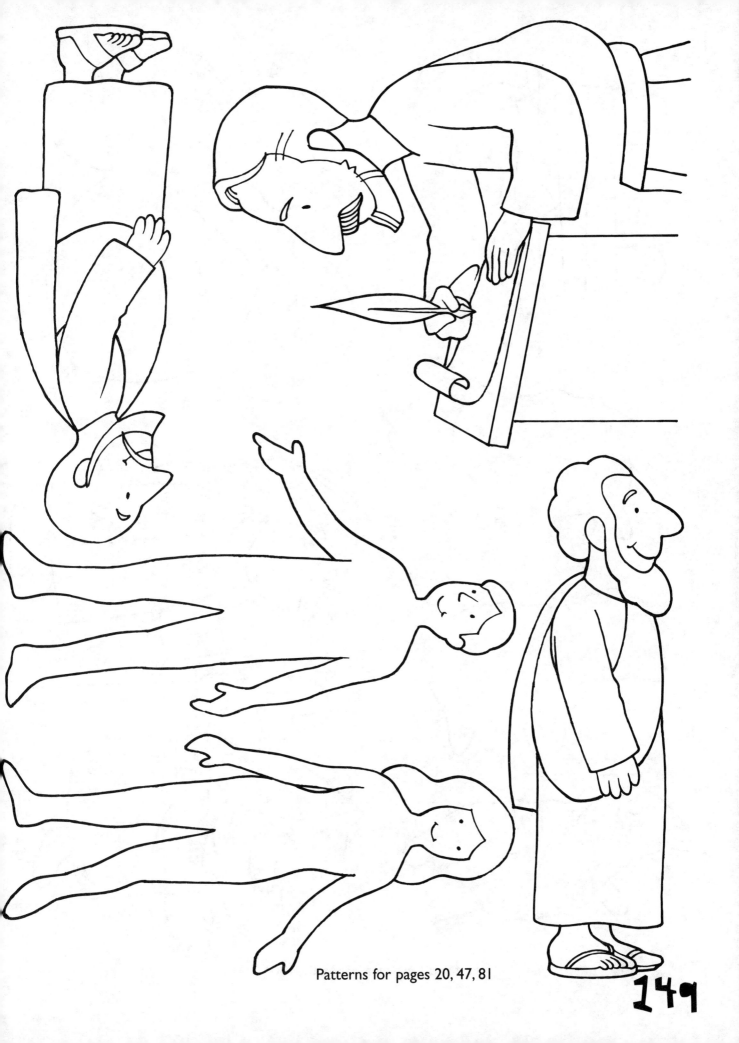

Patterns for pages 20, 47, 81

149

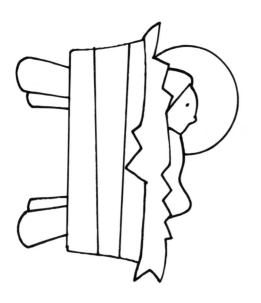

150

Patterns for pages 23, 73, 86, 130

Patterns for pages 17, 43, 44

151

152

154

Patterns for pages 99, 124, 130, 138

Patterns for pages 13, 101, 102, 141, 143

155

156

Patterns for pages 21, 118, 129, 138, 139

Patterns for pages 117, 118, 138

157

Index

2's and 3's Syllabus

AUTUMN, YEAR ONE: GOD'S GIFTS
Unit One: The World God Made (page 8)
Unit Two: The People God Made (page 9)
Unit Three: God's Loving Care (page 10)

WINTER, YEAR ONE: JESUS, OUR FRIEND
Unit One: Jesus Comes to Earth (page 11)
Unit Two: Jesus Is God's Son (page 12)
Unit Three: Jesus Loves Us (page 13)

SPRING, YEAR ONE: WHAT GOD WANTS US TO BE
Unit One: We Are Thankful (page 14)
Unit Two: Helpers for Jesus (page 15)
Unit Three: Learning About Me (page 16)

SUMMER, YEAR ONE: HOW WE SHOW OUR LOVE FOR GOD
Unit One: We Learn from the Bible (page 17)
Unit Two: We Talk to God (page 18)
Unit Three: We Help Others (page 19)

AUTUMN, YEAR TWO: GOD WHO MADE US
Unit One: God Is Great (page 20)
Unit Two: God Is Love (page 21)
Unit Three: God Is Good (page 22)

WINTER, YEAR TWO: JESUS, GOD'S SON
Unit One: God Sends His Son (page 23)
Unit Two: Jesus Grows Up (page 24)
Unit Three: God's Son, Jesus (page 25)

SPRING, YEAR TWO: JESUS WHO LOVES US
Unit One: Jesus Is Our Friend (page 26)
Unit Two: Jesus Is Close to Us (page 27)
Unit Three: We Are Jesus' Helpers (page 28)

SUMMER, YEAR TWO: MAKING GOOD CHOICES
Unit One: Learning to Love God (page 29)
Unit Two: Learning to Share (page 30)
Unit Three: Learning to Help (page 31)

4's and 5's/Primary Syllabus

AUTUMN, YEAR ONE: WORSHIP GOD
Unit One: He Made Everything (page 34)
Unit Two: He Keeps His Promises (page 35)
Unit Three: He Cares (page 36)

WINTER, YEAR ONE: FOLLOW JESUS
Unit One: He Is the Son of God (page 37)
Unit Two: He Is a Friend (page 38)
Unit Three: He Is a Friend to Everyone (page 39)

SPRING, YEAR ONE: TELL ABOUT JESUS
Unit One: Learn About Jesus (page 40)
Unit Two: Tell Others About Jesus (page 41)
Unit Three: Tell About Jesus When it Is Difficult (page 42)

SUMMER, YEAR ONE: CHOOSE TO DO RIGHT
Unit One: Do Right (page 43)
Unit Two: Do Right When it Is Hard (page 44)
Unit Three: Do What God Says Is Right (page 45)

AUTUMN, YEAR TWO: GOD IS GREAT
Unit One: He Helps People (page 46)
Unit Two: He Is Powerful (page 47)
Unit Three: He Hears Prayers (page 48)

WINTER, YEAR TWO: JESUS IS OUR LEADER
Unit One: Celebrate Jesus' Birth (page 49)
Unit Two: Jesus Is the Son of God (page 50)
Unit Three: Jesus Is Our Teacher (page 51)

SPRING, YEAR TWO: JESUS IS SPECIAL
Unit One: Jesus Is Special (page 52)
Unit Two: Jesus Is Alive (page 53
Unit Three: Jesus' Special Church (page 54)

SUMMER, YEAR TWO: I WILL DO RIGHT
Unit One: Do Right Wherever You Are (page 55)
Unit Two: Do What Is Right (page 56)
Unit Three: Do Right at Home and School (page 57)

Middler Syllabus

Preteen Syllabus